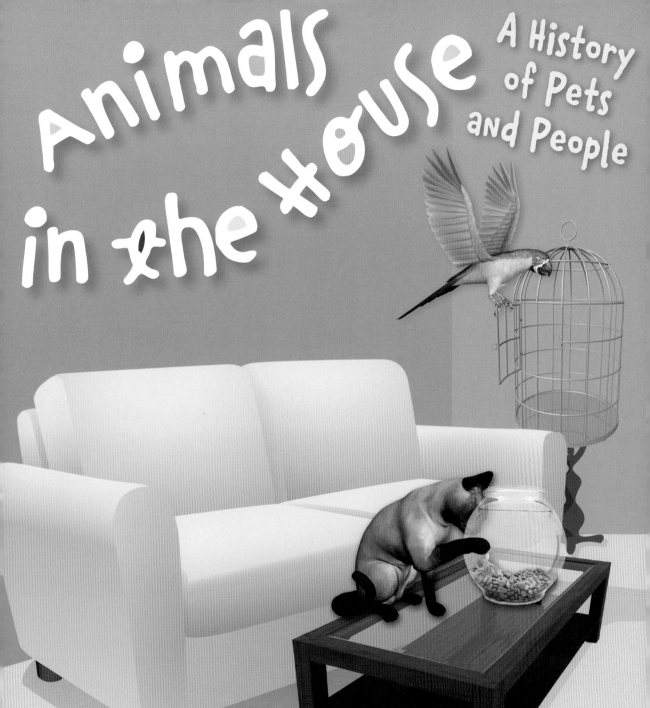

Animals in the House

A History of Pets and People

Sheila Keenan

SCHOLASTIC NONFICTION
An imprint of
SCHOLASTIC

For my darling Kevin

Many thanks to *editor extraordinaire,* Kate Waters, for all her great insights. Thanks also to Brenda Murray for her helpful editorial work and to Kay Petronio for the snazzy design.

Image research by Kevin Callahan and Kay Petronio
Book design by Kay Petronio
Printed in Singapore   46
First printing, April 2007

Library of Congress Cataloging-in-Publication Data
Keenan, Sheila.
Animals in the House: a history of pets and people / by Sheila Keenan.
p. cm.
Includes bibliographical references.
ISBN 10: 0-439-69286-5
ISBN 13: 978-0-439-69286-1
(alk. paper)
1. Pets—History—Juvenile literature. 2. Human-animal relationships—History—Juvenile literature.
I. Title.
SF416.2.K434 2007
636.088'7'09—dc22
2005047056

10 9 8 7 6 5 4 3 2
09 10 11

In loving memory of **Will Bennett**

monkey & corbie

Front cover: Alan Hettinger, Chris Lawrence, Marcin Laskowski/iStockphoto.com; Back cover: Photodisc.com; Flaps: Shutterstock.com; Page 1: Shutterstock.com, Marcin Laskowski/Stockphoto.com; Page 2: Shutterstock.com; Page 3: Shutterstock.com; Page 4: Fotosearch.com, Clipart.com; Page 6: Shutterstock.com, Jaimie D. Travis/iStockphoto.com, PictureQuest.com; Page 7: Clipart.com; Page 8: Clipart.com; Page 9: Shutterstock.com; Page 10: Fanelie Rosier/iStockphoto.com, Shutterstock.com; Page 11: Shutterstock.com; Page 12: Shutterstock.com; Page 13: Clipart.com; Page 14: Shutterstock.com; Page 15: Shutterstock.com, Fabian Guignard/iStockphoto.com; Page 16: Royalty-Free/Corbis; Page 17: Richard T. Nowitz/Corbis; Page 18: Shutterstock.com, Shin Yoshino/Minden Pictures; Page 19: Valley of the Kings, Thebes, Egypt/Bridgeman Art Library; Page 20: Shutterstock.com; Page 21: Steve Greer/iStockphoto.com, Shutterstock.com; Page 22: The Granger Collection, New York; Page 23: Shutterstock.com; Page 24: Kevin Russ/iStockphoto.com, Shutterstock.com; Page 25: Clipart.com; Page 26: The Ancient Art & Architecture Collection Ltd.; Page 27: Shutterstock.com; Page 28: Snark/Art Resource, NY, Shutterstock.com; Page 29: Dover Publications, Inc.; Page 30: Hulton-Deutsch Collection/Corbis; Page 31: Dover Publications, Inc.; Page 32: PoodlesRock/Corbis, Dover Publications, Inc.; Page 33: Dover Publications, Inc.; Page 34: NewsCom.com; Page 35: Sea-Monkey Aquarium; Page 36: Haruyoshi Yamaguchi/Corbis, www.lapetitemaison.com; Page 37: www.koko.org; Pages 38–39: Shutterstock.com; Page 40: Erich Lessing/Art Resource, NY; Pages 40–41: Clipart.com; Page 41: Ashmolean Museum, University of Oxford, UK/Bridgeman Art Library; Page 42: Mike Powell/Getty Images; Page 43: Shutterstock.com, Clipart.com; Page 44: Shutterstock.com; Page 45: Alinari Archives/Corbis, Clipart.com; Page 46: Shutterstock.com; Page 47: Corbis, Shutterstock.com; Page 48: Reuters/Corbis; Page 49: Shutterstock.com; Page 50: Shutterstock.com, Yann Arthus-Bertrand/Corbis; Page 51: Getty Images, Shutterstock.com, Yann Arthus-Bertrand/Corbis, James Levin; Page 52: Shutterstock.com; Page 53: Shutterstock.com; Page 54: Raymond Truelove, Todd Taulman, Kevin Russ/iStockphoto.com, Shutterstock.com; Page 55: Justin Horrocks/iStockphoto.com; Pages 56–57: Shutterstock.com; Pages 58–59: Corbis; Page 60: Getty Images; Page 61: The Ancient Art & Architecture Collection Ltd., Justin Horrocks/iStockphoto.com; Page 62: Werner Forman/Art Resource, NY; Page 63: Dover Publications, Inc.; Page 64: Keren Su, Robert Dowling/Corbis; Page 65: Shutterstock.com; Page 66: Justin Horrocks/iStockphoto.com; Page 67: Yann Arthus-Bertrand/Corbis; Page 68: Time Life Pictures/Getty Images, The Ancient Art & Architecture Collection Ltd.; Page 69: Hulton-Deutsch Collection/Corbis; Page 70: Tim Davis/Corbis, Getty Images; Page 71: Shutterstock.com, Bettmann/Corbis; Page 72: Forestier Yves/Corbis, Shutterstock.com; Page 73: Shutterstock.com; Page 74: Getty Images; Page 75: Bettmann, Underwood & Underwood/Corbis; Page 76: John Springer Collection/Corbis, Shutterstock.com; Page 77: Alex Hinds, Sheila Broumley/iStockphoto.com, PictureHistory.com; Page 78: Bettmann/Corbis; Page 79: Bettmann/Corbis; Page 80: Shutterstock.com; Page 81: Shutterstock.com, Wee Gan Peng/iStockphoto.com; Page 82: Shutterstock.com; Page 83: Shutterstock.com; Page 84: Photodisc.com, Dover Publications, Inc.; Page 85: Tamara Bauer/iStockphoto.com, Shutterstock.com; Page 86: Shutterstock.com; Page 87: Shutterstock.com; Page 88: Linda Bucklin/iStockphoto.com, Shutterstock.com; Page 89: Shutterstock.com; Page 90: Dover Publications, Inc., Clipart.com; Page 91: Dover Publications, Inc.; Page 92: Corbis, Shutterstock.com; Page 93: Li Kim Goh/iStockphoto.com, Shutterstock.com; Page 94: British Museum, London, UK/The Bridgeman Art Library; Page 95: Shutterstock.com; Page 96: Corbis; Page 97: Shutterstock.com; Page 98: Getty Images; Page 99: Shutterstock.com; Page 100: Shutterstock.com, Julie de Leseleuc/iStockphoto.com; Page 101: Clipart.com, Getty Images; Page 103: Ryan Tacay/iStockphoto.com; Page 104: Shutterstock.com; Page 105: Judy Watt, Dan Brandenburg/iStockphoto.com; Page 106: Ashmolean Museum, University of Oxford, UK/Bridgeman Art Library; Page 107: Bettmann/Corbis; Page 108: Getty Images, Shutterstock.com; Page 109: Dover Publications, Inc.

Contents

SPLASH!

Introduction

Is there something scampering, purring, swimming, or slithering in your home?

If so, you're not alone.

There are millions of people like you—they own pets, too.

All around the world, people are playing with their dogs, petting their cats, whistling along with their birds, feeding their fish, or going for a stroll with a pet rat in their pocket.

If you walk into two-thirds of the homes in the United States, you'll find animals living there, and not just the human kind. In fact, pets actually outnumber people!

People in the U.S.:
290,000,000

Pets in the U.S.:
377,800,000

Pets come in all sizes, shapes, and species. We like them large and small. We like them with fur, fins, flippers, or scales. In fact, we *love* our pets, whether they have two feet, or four feet, or no feet.

Any animal can be treated as a pet, and at one time or another, most have been. The Egyptian queen Cleopatra gave the Roman emperor Julius Caesar a giraffe. The 16th-century pope Leo X had a dancing white elephant. A badger, a bear, a blue macaw, guinea pigs, a hen, a hyena, a lizard, an owl, a pig, a pony, a rabbit, a one-legged rooster, snakes, and assorted cats and dogs have all been pets at the White House. There are even 12,000 "pet" tigers

pets at the white House

Pet Ownership

74 million dogs

90 million cats

9 million reptiles

192 million fish

17 million small animals

17 million birds

*Don't try this at home. Wild animals like big cats or primates should not be pets. The scientific community and animal welfare groups will tell you the same thing: It is dangerous, unfair to the animals, and environmentally harmful to take animals out of their habitats and bring them home. That's why they're called wild. Stick to domesticated animals and choose pets that are bred in captivity. Or visit a rescue league and adopt one of the millions of animals abandoned every year.

in the United States today; one lived in a New York City apartment until it mauled its owner.*

Most of our pets tend to be less ferocious, though. In the United States, people own nearly 90 million cats, 74 million dogs, 17 million birds, almost 17 million small animals, and 9 million reptiles. Added together, that's still fewer pets than the 192 million fish swimming in homes across the country!

Pick Me! Pick Me!

Most people have strong opinions about animals, especially pets. Dogs usually lead in animal popularity polls; rats make the "least-liked" lists. Scientists have studied these attitudes about animals and found that:

- People like animals that are useful.

- Size counts: People generally find bigger animals more attractive than smaller ones.

- Strong communication skills are a plus. People choose animals they feel they can communicate with as pets. That's why so many people have cats and dogs. (Be honest: It's hard to get a response out of a hermit crab, isn't it?)

- People really go for cute, warm, and fuzzy. (Think about a puppy. Now think about a pig. Which one would *you* cuddle?)

When you get a pet, you voluntarily enter a full-time relationship. Now you have an animal to feed, which

YES!

could mean tapping a few flakes into the goldfish bowl, or providing live mice for a boa. You have an animal with bathroom needs, which could mean a quick flush after a toilet-trained ferret, or trudging through freezing rain while your dog finds the exact right spot to lift its leg. You have a whole new shopping list, which could include food bowls, water bottles, collars, carriers, toys, and fresh supplies of kibble or canned glop.

Chihuahua

Props to Pets

Pets are now a *37-billion*-dollar business in the United States alone. That's how much U.S. pet owners spent on their animals in 2004, not counting the cost of the pet itself. Today's pet owners carry photos of their beloved animals in their wallets. Several recent studies show that between 70% and 84% of them consider their pets members of the family. And they care for pets like family. That doesn't just mean providing food and shelter. That means birthday celebrations! Holiday presents! Phone calls home when they're traveling! Maybe even a postcard or a souvenir! More than a third of pet owners polled agree they do one, sometimes all, of these things for their favorite critters.

Pug

Too much? Maybe not!

Research into the effects of pet ownership has been going on since the 1970s. The findings? Pets are good medicine!

 People with pets live longer and make fewer doctor visits.

 Pet owners have a much better chance of surviving heart attacks.

 Pets can help lower stress levels and blood pressure.

Pets can help fight depression.

Therapists have successfully used pets in working with abused or troubled children, depressed or institutionalized people, and people who are withdrawn because of autism. You can now find visiting pets in nursing homes; they've been shown to have a positive effect on the health and spirits of seniors.

It makes sense. Pets accept you as you are. They don't wonder if you're the right breed, have enough money, or show well. They'll slobber all over you, sit in your lap, perch on your shoulder, or go about their fascinating animal business, no matter who you are. That's why we love them!

Spaniel

WOOF!

Born to Be Wild

PETS INVENTED

Watching a pet makes you wonder: Just how did animals come out of the wild and move into our hearts and homes? How exactly did animals become pets?

You won't find a date for "world's first pet born" or "pets invented" in any history book. The idea of keeping animals as pets developed over time...a really *long* time. And before people could even think about animals as companions, they had to figure out how to domesticate them.

Domestication means breeding animals so that they keep some characteristics and lose others over generations. Naturally, the characteristics kept are the ones that make animals the most useful and the least harmful to human beings. Domestication turns wild animals into working animals. You want to be able to milk them, ride them, or use them as pack or draft animals. You want them to guard you, kill vermin in your home, or help you herd or hunt.

Not all animals are created equal when it comes to domestication. Think tiger: solitary, big teeth, sharp claws, leaps and kills with a swift bite to the neck...definitely *not* a good candidate!

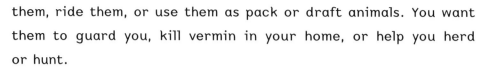

DOMESTICATION TO-DO LIST

NO! ✗

YES! ✓

My Kind of Animal

Most of the animals that people successfully domesticated share these traits. They are hardy and not likely to die soon after they are caught. They breed easily in captivity. If you're going to domesticate an animal, you want to make sure its young grow up into useful beasts *fast*. Time is money...and animal feed!

You definitely want a "social" animal. Social animals naturally live in groups and have a leader. When you domesticate them, you're basically regrouping them and making yourself the leader of the pack or herd. Animals like this are easier to tend, another strong point. You want your domesticated animals to follow orders, not trample you! That's why you also need breeds with good dispositions. When was the last time you saw someone saddle up a zebra? Zebras are much more likely to bite you than horses are.

Most domesticated animals are also herbivores because it's cheaper and easier to feed plant eaters. (Dogs don't count—everyone knows they'll eat anything!)

While studying how early humans lived, archaeologists have also been digging up the dirt on when and where animals were first domesticated. Recent DNA analysis of dog remains suggest their ancestors may have come from east Asia, rather than Europe or the Middle East as has long been thought. Prehistoric remains unearthed in Cyprus suggest that cats may have been domesticated 9,500 years ago; up until now, the ancient Egyptians have been getting all the credit for taming wild felines about 4,000 years ago. Goat bones found in Iran and dating back 10,000 years put that four-footer near the top of the domestication chart.

Cyprus

who Let the Dogs In?

Dogs, the first domesticated animals, had some wild ancient ancestors: wolves. When prehistoric people set up camp or later built settlements, they inevitably created garbage. Wolves lurked, munching on whatever shells, bones, or scraps people tossed away. Over time these wolves, though still wary, may have gotten used to the two-legged, talking animals in their midst.

Wolves that lived near people may have survived at a higher rate than their fellow members of *Canis lupus* because they scrounged food from the humans. Their offspring would be less feral or wild. People kept and bred these wolves. Early people may have caught wolf cubs in the wild and tamed and bred them, too.

Eventually, some generation of skulking wolves became domesticated dogs. DNA studies show that dogs were around as long as 15,000 years ago. Fossil finds of domestic dogs in Iraq date from 14,000 years ago. The first dogs in North America may have come with the hardy hunter-gatherers who crossed over from Asia via the Bering Strait.

Psss, Psss, Here, Puss

You can see why people would want dogs around. They'll bite your enemies, herd your other domesticated animals, maybe even pull your sled. But cats? Why bother domesticating them?

In a word: rats.

No one is quite sure when wild cats became domesticated. One reason is that it's hard to tell the difference between the bones of wild cats and those of the early domesticated cats. It's possible that wild cats were hanging around prehistoric Neolithic humans, hunting the snakes and rodents attracted to their grain or garbage. When people moved from hunting and gathering to farming, they raised crops and stored grains. Grain warehouses were like smorgasbords for rats and mice—and these vermin were like takeout for cats.

All-American Cats

Cats are overlooked American heroes.

Without domesticated cats, the early American colonies would have been overrun with rats. Pennsylvania had a major rodent epidemic in the 1740s and actually had to import cats. It would have been difficult for settlers in the Midwest to farm if they didn't have cats to keep squirrels and rodents from eating their crops and seeds. Ditto for the pioneers trying to make it all the way west via wagon train. Nineteenth-century gold rush miners were willing to pay for a good mouser that kept the rats from biting them at night. One entrepreneur bought a hundred or so cats for a dime apiece, shipped them to San Francisco, and sold them to the miners for $20 each. Cats even helped out the U.S. Postal Service. Post office cats kept vermin from gnawing the mailbags.

Beast of Burden or Best Friend?

Just because animals were domesticated didn't mean they automatically became pets. Remember: *animal* ≡ *pet* is an equation that took people a long time to solve. *Animal* ≡ *worker* ＋ *companion* ＋ *food-on-foot* was more like it. For thousands of years, animals had overlapping relationships with their owners. Sure, you might pet a herding dog affectionately, even let it a bit closer to the fire, but if times got tough and you got hungry, well...

The status of animals plays a big part in the history of pets. That status is directly tied to what different people in different times thought about their fellow creatures. And what people thought about animals influenced how they lived with them.

together forever

Prehistoric people may have recognized that animals were good for something besides food and fur: They make nice pets, too. The proof may have been buried in a Paleolithic site found in Israel in 1978. Inside the 12,000-year-old tomb was a human skeleton, its left hand resting on the shoulder of a puppy skeleton. Man's best friend? Could be. (Actually, the human remains are those of an elderly woman.)

In 2004, archaeologists found a Neolithic grave on the island of Cyprus that held polished stone axes, flint tools, and a human skeleton. There was a complete cat skeleton buried close by. The skeletons were buried symmetrically; both their heads faced west. Stray cat? Unlikely. Special cat? Likely. The cat may have been killed as part of the prehistoric ritual burial of its owner.

The bones of a dog being uncovered from an archaeological site in Ashqelon, Israel.

Ten-thousand-year-old stone or clay figures of cats have also been found in Israel, Syria, and Turkey, a fact that suggests cats meant something to the ancient people in these places.

Ancient Animal Lovers

Ancient people lived very close to their animals and acknowledged their importance. In many tribal societies, from Australia to the Americas, there wasn't a sharp division between the world of animals and the world of humans. Animals were honored as creators, ancestors, messengers of the gods, or great sources of wisdom and insight. They had important roles in tribal art and ritual. And some of them became pets.

Pet keeping has been recorded in nearly every traditional society around the world. Mesoamericans kept raccoons as house pets; so did some North American Indians. Brazilian Indians loved birds, particularly the beautiful parrots they tamed as pets. The Aboriginal people in Australia kept dingoes, dogs that slept and ate with their human owners; the North American Comanches were devoted to their canines.

Parrot

Dingo

Egyptians: Definitely Animal People

An Egyptian god or goddess was often shown with a human body and an animal head. The animal's traits symbolized the deity.

Nobody in the ancient world matched the Egyptians when it came to living with animals. Dogs, cats, cattle, crocodiles, ibises, hippos, snakes, and scarabs were all revered. They led pampered lives in sacred temples (or sacred pools, depending on the beast).

The ancient Egyptians didn't consider themselves superior to their fellow creatures. They believed animals were representatives or reincarnations of gods and goddesses. The pharaohs were famous animal collectors and established royal zoological gardens filled with exotic animals. Egyptians of all classes kept a variety of pets; cats and dogs were the most popular.

On a Scale of 1 to 10...

The ancient Greeks believed in sharing their world with animals. They thought if you mistreated an animal, the gods would punish you. Besides, you never know: A swan could turn out to be the great god Zeus in disguise!

During the 4th century BC, the brilliant Greek philosopher and naturalist Aristotle wrote that human beings were animals, but were the only animals that could reason and had souls. That put us a rung up on his *scala natura*, or Ladder of Nature. This ladder theory explained how everything in nature was arranged, from high to low: gods, humans, higher mammals, all the way down to insects, etc. It suggested that animals existed for the sake of human beings and for what they could provide us.

The Greeks loved watching parades of exotic animals brought into their cities from foreign lands. They lavished attention on their horses. They tamed monkeys and birds. They were especially fond of dogs and were the first to breed sheepdogs. Some Greeks carried small dogs around with them to public places like the baths or the market. World conqueror Alexander the Great even named a captured city after his great hound, Peritas.

All Hail, Rome!

The Romans agreed with the Greeks that people were the dominant animal species. As they marched around conquering the ancient world, the Romans rounded up all kinds of exotic animals: lions and tigers, giraffes, hippos, elephants, and rhinos. Many were shipped back to Rome for the wealthy to keep in their private zoos. The unluckier animals ended up fighting in bloody, gruesome spectacles witnessed by thousands at Roman arenas.

When they weren't killing off animals, Romans enjoyed their company as pets. Dogs, from Maltese to Mastiffs, were very popular. The Romans also trained monkeys and birds and kept fish. Cages of nightingales hung in their beautiful villa courtyards, where fish swam in their *piscinari*, or tanks. Some fish were bred and stocked as food, but others were treated as pets. One upper-class Roman matron even put gold earrings on her favorite finned one.

And God said, Let us make man in our image, after our likeness: and let them have dominion over the fish of the sea, and over the fowl of the air, and over the cattle, and over all the earth, and over every creeping thing that creepeth upon the earth.
—The Bible, Genesis 1

MUSCLE OR MEAT

During biblical times and the Christian era that followed in much of the Western world, animal inferiority was widely accepted. The Bible made it clear that people were in charge and animals were created for our use, although you weren't supposed to be cruel to them. Animals were considered domesticated beasts, rather than pets. There are only 41 mentions of dogs in the Bible, most of them insulting; the poor cat is left out entirely!

Islamic writings also suggest that animals are part of all

creation, but still can be freely used by human beings. For centuries, people thought animals existed to serve—as muscle or meat.

Still, some animals escaped work or the dinner plate and became household favorites. Many Christian popes owned dogs or cats, among other pets. Muhammad himself is said to have been very fond of his cat, Meuzza. A story of the Prophet says he once sliced off his sleeve rather than disturb Meuzza, who was nestled in it.

we Are All Animals

Not everyone in the world puts people above "soulless" animals. The relationship among living things is not so vertical to Buddhists, Hindus, and members of other Eastern religions. They believe all forms of life are part of a sacred unity. They also believe in reincarnation, the cycle of birth, death, and rebirth. These incarnations could take all forms, including animal; therefore, animals must be honored and respected. Usually animals are at the lower end of the reincarnation cycle, though. It's a stage you want to work your way out of on the path to enlightenment.

Dog

pet

Yorkshire Terrier

The word *pet* only entered the English language around 1508, thousands of years after animals had been tamed, trained, and often pampered.

Courtly Critters in the Middle Ages & Renaissance

Many medieval people would have questioned why you'd want to keep and feed an idle animal like a pet. A nonworking animal was pointless and maybe even the devil's partner. Animals were still on the lower rungs of the Ladder of Nature. Then again, in feudal times, so were most people.

Not so in the royal courts of the Middle Ages and later the Renaissance. There, kings, queens, noblemen and noblewomen, and their animals lived pampered, privileged lives. Some royal animals, like hunting dogs, horses, and falcons, still worked for their masters. But the aristocracy also owned real pets, animals they kept solely for companionship, entertainment, or prestige.

In medieval China, royal dogs wore gold or silver collars. During the Tang dynasty (618–907), the imperial rulers bestowed official ranks on their Chow dogs. The Chows got the best seats at court. They made grand entrances to music, wearing earrings with tinkly little bells and gold- or silver-belled collars. Animals also attended the royal court in Ghana in the 11th century, where the African king's dogs wore gold and silver collars.

European aristocrats spent fortunes on their pets. Dogs ran around in gold, silver, pearl, or ruby collars. Cats wore velvet coats and were sprinkled with perfume.

Cats and dogs wandered the royal dining halls, where they were often fed sweets and rich foods by hand. Noblewomen kissed and cooed over the little lapdogs they carried around with them, tucked into their sleeves or necklines.

Court pets had all kinds of privileges. They had servants, feeders, and grooms. They were allowed to sleep in the royal bedrooms and romp, dirty paws and all, on the handmade satin and linen sheets. They trotted across dining tables and got underfoot. They weren't housebroken and roamed the castles and palaces, acting like, well, uh... animals!

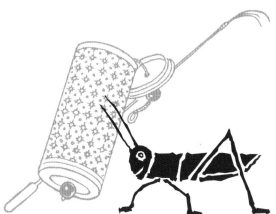

Many Chinese people kept crickets and katydids as pets. The nobility kept these singing insects in beautiful cages made of gold, jade, ivory, or buffalo horn; the common folk kept their chirpers in gourds or bamboo cages.

How cute! Feeding a pup by hand...but this dog may not be as pampered as it looks. Some dogs in the 15th century were used as food testers to make sure nobody was serving poisonous dishes to the king.

Pets as calling cards

Pets were given and received as symbolic tokens. Marrying a fellow royal you've never met? Send a cute pet by way of introduction (or bring your own to keep you company in an unwelcoming foreign court). Want to make sure you're well received at court? Send a new breed of puppy to your king or queen. Need to keep a royal mistress happy? Acknowledge a potential ally? Celebrate a treaty or trade agreement? Curry favor? A pet was the way to go.

Pets were also often the best friends and only comfort for royal women and children who were trapped by the strict, lonely formality of court life.

Living, Yelping Status Symbols

Over time, pet owning at court became more and more conspicuous—and competitive.

The second half of the 15th century was a great age of exploration. Ships sailed out from Europe to the east and west and returned (*if* they returned) with all sorts of treasures and trade goods, including animals. Colorful parrots became the "must-have" pets for the status-conscious wealthy, especially after Columbus presented two of these beautiful parrots to his benefactor, Queen Isabella of Spain. Portuguese sailors brought home little Japanese Chins, the royal dogs of Japan. Guinea pigs were all the rage at court once England's Queen Elizabeth I was seen with hers.

Guinea Pig

In European royal drawing rooms of the 16th and 17th centuries, lords, ladies, kings, and queens set off royal canine fads. Various "toy" dogs such as Bolognese Spaniels; dainty, butterfly-eared Papillons; fluffy Toy Poodles; and Pekingese and Maltese became the height of fashion. The European aristocracy had their portraits painted with the petite pups in their arms or at their feet gazing up adoringly. The 16th-century French king Henry III often tied a small basket around his neck with ribbons, his favorite little white Bichon Frise snuggled inside. King and dogs went to council meetings and received ambassadors together.

Bichon Frise

The Bichon Frise has a double coat, which makes it look like a little cotton ball. Medieval Italian, Spanish, and French nobles were crazy about this breed.

> *Cogito ergo sum.*
> I think,
> therefore I am.

Are Animals Like Us?

French philosopher, mathematician, and dog owner René Descartes was one of the great thinkers of the early 17th century. He argued that truth had to be proven by evidence or reasoning. "I think, therefore I am" is his most famous line.

Descartes wrote that animals were soulless machines. They were automatons that worked like clocks. And what made animals "work" were gases that flowed through them and moved their muscles. They didn't think, choose, act, or feel.

The fallout from Descartes' philosophy was that many people didn't worry about animal cruelty or hesitate to use live animals in science experiments. Ironically, these science experiments would lead to better treatment of animals. The more scientists learned about the circulatory, nervous, and other body systems, the more it seemed that natural laws applied to humans *and* animals.

> Bow-wow! Me, too!

Boxer

the 18th century: Need class? Get a Pet.

Pet owning became more democratic in the 18th century. There were still plenty of pets at court. Prussian king Frederick the Great was devoted to his miniature Italian Greyhounds, which had their own horse-drawn carriage. Queen Marie Antoinette of France's little pooch slept in a lavish golden dog bed with silk and velvet pillows.

But there was a growing middle class in Europe who thought owning a pet was classy. Now you could also find pets in the homes of merchants and manufacturers.

Pets lived in the American colonies, too. Two dogs, a Mastiff and an English Spaniel, sailed over on the *Mayflower* in 1620. By 1703, Boston was so overrun by dogs, you had to prove your worth to become a dog owner. You needed an annual income of 20 pounds; even if you had it, there was a one-pooch-per-household limit. Philadelphians ruled there could be no "Great Dogs" within the city. And colonial pet keeping went beyond the standard pooches and pusses. With so many amazing animals around, why limit yourself? Colonial boys tamed and kept squirrels as pets; colonial girls were praised for training small birds. There are colonial accounts of tamed deer and pet beavers that followed their masters around like dogs. And a dog was always a great foot warmer in chilly colonial churches.

the Victorians: mad about Animals

Pets really became members of the family during the 19th century. The critter-loving middle class had become more prominent than ever. And new science theories changed the way people thought about animals.

This era is named after Queen Victoria, one of the biggest animal-loving monarchs of all time. Victoria ruled Great Britain from 1837 to 1901. She owned 88 pets during her lifetime, mostly dogs, and had portraits painted of every one of her pampered canines.

Middle-class Victorians were very sentimental about animals, especially pets. They thought animals were unspoiled, innocent, and in need of protection. Pets were used for moral instruction. Dogs stood for unquestionable loyalty; cats were perfect examples of neatness. Animal families, with an attentive dog or cat guarding its roly-

Queen Victoria and one of her favorite dogs.

poly pups or playful kittens, were symbols of the ideal, "natural" human family. The latest ladies' magazines were full of sentimental animal stories and poems. Decorative prints of animals fawning over one another or their masters hung in many Victorian parlors.

Most people in the 19th century believed human beings had God-given rule over animals. But some scientists and philosophers now argued that perhaps people had duties toward animals, too. Some said this because they recognized that animals could indeed feel pain and suffer. Others believed that people didn't morally owe animals anything, but that being cruel to them led to being cruel to humans. Naturalist Charles Darwin inflamed these discussions when he published his books on evolution, beginning with *On the Origin of Species* in 1859. His influential work changed the way most people looked at the natural world and their place in it.

my Dear Little Pet

All of these new ideas convinced the middle-class Victorians that they were right: Owning pets and being kind to animals were signs of being cultivated and genteel. People had their photographs taken with their beloved animals. Promenading with your pet was a regular Sunday activity for the middle and upper classes. People even called one another "pet," as a nickname or an endearment.

Pets show off

Official cat and dog shows were first staged in the 1800s; by the end of the 19th century, animal "fancier" clubs had been established. Groups like the Westminster Kennel Club and the American Cat Association had strict rules about breeds, membership, and showing animals. Animal protection societies were also formed. Henry Bergh, a wealthy New Yorker, founded the American Society for the Prevention of Cruelty to Animals in 1866. The ASPCA helped create and enforce laws that banned the mistreatment of animals. (Seven years later, in a court case about child abuse, Bergh argued that these laws applied to kids, too, since a child is an animal. He won. Bergh founded the American Association for the Prevention of Cruelty to Children in 1874 and sparked a movement for children's rights.)

Serena Williams and friend

Pets in the modern world

By the 20th century, keeping animals as pets was widely accepted. Pet shops opened up all across the country. New scientific studies in animal intelligence, behavior, and communication started. And pets became media hounds.

Animals had inspired artists and writers for centuries; now they became stars in movies and later television shows. Celebrities and politicians knew it was good publicity to be photographed with a favorite feline or hound.

Pets set off crazes: Everybody wanted a Collie once Lassie started barking on the nation's TV screens. The most unlikely critters became popular pets in the 1950s and 1960s. Ant farms were marketed as "a living TV screen that will keep you interested for hours!" Kids clamored for weird pets like Sea Monkeys.

Modern pets didn't even have to be alive! In 1975, Gary Dahl of California "invented" the pet rock. Yup! That's what it was, just a *rock*. He sold a million of them, along with a pet-rock care handbook. Tamagotchi, a Japanese invention, was a huge hit in the late 1990s. This electronic gizmo on a key ring was a virtual pet that would hatch and grow on a little screen—*if* you pressed buttons to feed it, clean it, and play with it every time it beeped. If you didn't keep your Tamagotchi happy, it would "die."

Just add water and these brine shrimp eggs come to life! Sea Monkeys were the brainstorm of scientist Harold von Braunhut, who started selling packages of "Instant Life" through comic book ads.

the Pampered Pet of the 21st Century

Pets today are often treated as royally as the noble court animals of the past. You can buy them accessories and clothes, including

pajamas, tuxedos, tiaras, diamond collars, and fur coats. (Fur on fur? How weird is that!) There are lines of pet toiletries, from shampoos to mouthwash to breath mints to nail polish for dogs. You can arrange a play date, a photo shoot, a yoga class, a massage, or a therapy session for your beloved animal. You can vacation with your pet at hotels that welcome your pooch or puss with room service, guest collars, or pet treats. If your pet needs a

A doggy mud scrub

break on its own, you can send it to camp or a pet spa.

You can clean your dog at a self-service center that's like a car wash for pooches. You can buy poop-protective flight suits for your bird, so you don't have to watch your head when you let your pet bird out of its cage.

Is your cat bored lying around your apartment sleeping? Now you can pop in a feline DVD with footage of squirrels, birds, and fish so that your cat can pretend it's a hunter again. Does your dog need its own space? Why not build it a two-story mansion? Or a Swiss chalet? Or a French château?

It took a long time for people other than royals or the rich to start treating animals as pets. And, of course, not all animals became household pets in the same way. Let's take a look at the individual histories of our most popular animal friends.

A cool canine crib

Here, Kitty, Kitty

Koko and her kitty pal, All-Ball

Cleopatra had one named Charmain. President Ronald Reagan had one named Cleo. Even a trained gorilla owned one.

Koko, the gorilla that could speak in sign language, had two tailless Manx kittens. The gorilla named the first kitten All-Ball because it curled up like a ball of fur. All-Ball was killed by a car. Koko was so depressed that she was given a new kitten, which she named Lips-Lipstick.

Cats are purring, meowing, or clawing the furniture in more than 32 million households across the United States. They're America's number-one pet—even though we're talking about an animal that sleeps 13 hours a day and grooms itself a third of the time it's awake. Not to mention cats are basically untrainable and generally do as they please!

How a cat works

Mine, mine, mine!

A cat has scent glands on its forehead and the sides of its mouth. These glands release the puss's own personal perfume. That's why a cat rubs everything—and everybody—that it wants to label "mine."

My, what big eyes you have!

Cats have the biggest eyes in relationship to their body size of any animal. These big peepers have an iridescent layer of cells on the retina, which reflect light like a mirror. This helps cats see at night and makes their eyes glow. Cats can see in the dark six times better than people can.

Tiny organs inside the ear help the cat balance.

Sniff

A cat's sense of smell is ten times sharper than ours because a cat has millions more olfactory cells for processing smelly stuff. Cats also sniff their paws for odiferous information about the things they've been batting around.

Tight squeeze

Things up close look blurry to a cat—that's where having whiskers helps. Cat whiskers are coarse hairs with nerve endings that are sensitive to touch. Whiskers give the cat information about close objects. Cats also use their whiskers to detect movement and determine space. Cats can move the top and bottom rows of whiskers independently.

Clean machines

Cats use saliva and their rough tongues to lick dirt out of their fur. They lick their paws and use them as washcloths to clean their faces.

Cat fur can be as thick as 200 hairs per millimeter of skin. These hairs grow out of little sacs buried in the skin. When cats are frightened, they use their muscles to push these sacs out, which makes their hair stand on end. Scaredy-cats puff themselves up to look bigger and more intimidating.

A cat sweats through glands in its paws.

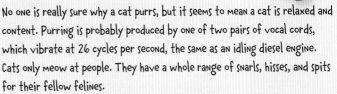

Psssst, Psssst, Psssst

Cats can swiftly rotate their ears nearly 180 degrees because they have 30–32 tiny muscles in them. They move their ears separately to catch different sounds at once. Cats can hear 65,000 vibrations per second, three times what we can and more than dogs.

Good vibrations

No one is really sure why a cat purrs, but it seems to mean a cat is relaxed and content. Purring is probably produced by one of two pairs of vocal cords, which vibrate at 26 cycles per second, the same as an idling diesel engine. Cats only meow at people. They have a whole range of snarls, hisses, and spits for their fellow felines.

The better to eat you with

A cat has 32 teeth: canines, incisors, and molars. It can move its lower jaw sideways, so it can really tear into its prey. A grinning cat isn't just happy to see you; it's sucking up smells. The Jacobson's organ at the top of its mouth filters odor from air the cat inhales.

Up in the air

Cat tails have around 20 bones, nearly 10% of the skeleton. The tail is amazingly flexible and helps the cat balance. It's also a big clue as to what a cat is thinking... or plotting. Tail up? The cat is glad to see you. Tail twitching? Could be interest, could be annoyance. Puffed-up tail? Somebody's angry; watch out!

A cat can jump five times as high as the length of its tail.

flexible felines

There are about 230 bones in a cat's skeleton (we have 206). These bones, and a cat's 14 kinds of muscles, make it a very flexible animal. That's why cats are famous for landing on their feet when they fall. Its spine twists so the cat's body rotates into the proper landing position. This flexibility is also why a cat can lick its own belly and do other weird contortions to clean itself.

The cat walk

Cats walk on their toes. Most cats have five toes on each front paw and four toes on each back paw. With a cat's retractable claws, there's no click, click, clicking around. A cat can silently sneak up on its prey, then—*flash!*—the claws spring out for the kill.

Hair-raisin'

The color, texture, and length of a cat's fur may tell you something about its breed. Flat or raised fur will tell you something about a cat's mood.

Left, right, left

Cats move both their left feet, then both their right feet. It's the stealthy, speedy way to go. Only camels and giraffes move this way, too. Most cats are either right-or left-pawed, just like people.

the Pharaoh's Puss

The ancient Egyptians were the first real cat people. They established the cult of the cat nearly 4,000 years ago. It's easy to see why people would think cats were powerful, even magical. Cats are very beautiful animals, with a mysterious air about them. They're nocturnal, and their unusual eyes let them see in the dark.

Felines were sacred to Bastet, the Egyptian moon goddess of pleasure, plenty, and fertility. Cats were also very useful rat catchers in Egypt's great grain storehouses. They were welcomed in Egyptian homes, too, where they were both mousers and pampered household pets, sometimes fed on milk-soaked bread.

Some Egyptian cats lived luxurious lives in temples of the gods, fed by high priests. Cat statues were bedecked in precious jewelry; rich Egyptian women painted on elaborate eye makeup, inspired by cat eyes.

A statue of Bastet

They wore charm bracelets with tiny feline figures dangling from them. Egyptian law forbade killing cats, among other animals.

By 950 BC, cat worship was frenzied. Hundreds of thousands of Egyptians sailed the Nile to the river city Bubastis for an annual festival. This celebration in Bastet's honor included wild music and riotous feasting, drinking, and dancing.

Cats were so revered that in 525 BC, Persian soldiers conquered the Egyptian city of Pelusium by holding live cats in front of them as they attacked the Egyptians. The Egyptians surrendered, rather than kill the cats.

This stone slab from ancient Egypt shows a man and woman adoring two cats meant to represent the sun god.

The Egyptian Mau is a modern breed of cat that resembles the sacred feline of the pharaohs. It is the only natural breed of spotted cat.

Cats Get Around

The Egyptians tried to keep cats for themselves, but seafaring Phoenicians probably smuggled a few felines out for trade. Cats are very fertile: One female cat and her offspring can produce 420,000 cats in seven years. So, by about 500 BC, domestic cats were living throughout the Middle East and the Mediterranean region. The Romans particularly admired the cat's independent nature. They emblazoned cats on their shields and military banners as a symbol of Rome's liberty. Trade routes took cats east to Asia by around 200 BC.

By the 5th century AD, cats had settled all across Europe, where a prized mouser fetched a good price. From convents to peasant cottages, people warmed up to felines as charming

Cats appear in many Chinese and Japanese legends and folktales. This tricolor Japanese *maneki neko* is a popular symbol of good luck and prosperity. *Maneki neko* means "beckoning cat."

pet companions *and* living mousetraps. Sixth-century Arabs also kept cats, particularly since Muhammad was believed to be very fond of his feline. Cats were the only animals allowed in Muslim mosques.

The first cats in Japan are said to have been five pure white kittens, born in 999 at the emperor's palace in Kyoto. Japanese aristocracy kept their cats pampered. They curled up on silk or satin pillows and were taken for walks on leashes in the garden. Meanwhile, the Japanese put up pictures and drawings of their cats, which they thought would be enough to keep mice away from their prized silkworms. The mice were unimpressed by the art and kept munching. The real cats were blamed: Good-bye, cushy life. In 1602, new laws put Japanese cats to work catching mice.

Cats may look sleepy, but everything about this animal, from its nose to its tail, makes it a good hunter. Even today's tabby is still a predator: Watch any kitten or cat and you'll see. They hunker down to the ground, haunches tight…then pounce! They race around chasing leaves, toys, or an invisible who-knows-what. Some scientific studies suggest that cats even hunt imaginary prey in their dreams!

Demon Cats, Deadly Rats

Christianity was widespread in Europe by the Middle Ages, but the church associated cats with ancient, pagan religions. The pope declared cats diabolical, or animals of the devil, in 1233. People still secretly kept cats, but it was dangerous to do so. You and your pet could be arrested for witchcraft!

Cats were accused of all kinds of black magic...especially black cats. Hundreds of thousands of cats were killed. Medieval celebrations often included cat torture. Felines were sacrificed on feast days, even tossed from towers. By 1400, cats had been nearly wiped out in western Europe.

Of course this murderous hatred of cats meant there were a lot more happy rodents scurrying around. There weren't enough cats left to kill the disease-carrying rats that spread from central Asia to Europe in the 14th century. The flea-bitten, plague-ridden rats ran free, spreading the Black Death. About 25 million people in Europe and 23 million in Asia died between 1346 and 1353.

The cat soon made a comeback.

Puss-in-Boats

In the 16th century, artists helped with cat appreciation. Masters like Leonardo da Vinci painted and drew beautiful cats at rest and play. Plump, contented, charming feline pets appeared in paintings of domestic scenes. By the end of the Renaissance, cats had nuzzled their way back into favor with the rich and the working class. Some people even thought about their cat's comfort: Isaac Newton, the gravity genius, invented a movable cat door so his pet could wander freely.

"The smallest of felines is a masterpiece!" –Leonardo da Vinci, Italian artist and scientist (1452–1519)

Puss-in-Boots went atraveling abroad, too. Cats were taken on board ships to keep vermin from eating precious cargo or supplies. Naturally, when the ships docked, so did some of the cats.

There were no known domestic cats in the Americas before the Europeans arrived, although ancient Peruvians may have tamed and kept wildcats such as the jaguarundi as pets. Domestic cats most likely traveled to the Americas with

Christopher Columbus and other European explorers and conquerors. There were probably cats on board the *Mayflower* with the Pilgrims. When these cats landed, they went their feline ways, making kittens and keeping pests away.

The Maine Coon cat is an American classic. It's one of the oldest breeds here. Many of the domestic cats that came to this continent grew larger, heavier, and furrier than their European ancestors, so they could survive the winters. Maine Coon cats can weigh 20 pounds, and their long, dense fur is waterproof.

Maine Coon

Pusses in the Parlor

Cats really became beloved household pets in the 18th and 19th centuries. Samuel Johnson, the great English writer who compiled the first dictionary, went to market every day to buy fresh oysters, which he hand-fed to his pet cat. Even the pope had a cat. The papal puss, Micetto, loved to nestle in the folds of Pope Leo XII's robes.

When Queen Victoria of Britain adopted a royal cat, a Persian, felines definitely became fashionable. So did cat breeding.

Persian cats are flat-faced felines with a superabundance of long, plush, soft hair. Trade caravans probably brought these fancy cats from Persia and Turkey to Europe in the 1600s. Persians became the must-have cat for wealthy Americans in the 1800s who followed European fads and fashions.

In 1871, the first official cat show was held in London's Crystal Palace. By the end of the century, there were several pedigree cat groups; the largest American one is the Cat Fanciers' Association (CFA).

The American Shorthair cat is the fancy version of your basic early-American mouser. It's the only other breed besides the Maine Coon that is native to the United States. This cat was deliberately bred in 1904, when people were worried that strong, robust shorthair cats would die out because fussy longhairs and exotics were *the* desirable cat breeds. Of course, now the American Shorthair is a fancy pedigree cat itself!

Mark Twain, the famous American author of *The Adventures of Huckleberry Finn*, gave his pet cats difficult names to teach his kids how to pronounce hard words. (Try calling a kitty, "Here, Blatherskite," or "Psss, psss, Zoraster"!)

American Shorthair

Socks Clinton
Chief Executive Cat

cats go to washington

If you're under stress, stroking a cat has now been shown to lower your blood pressure. Maybe President Abraham Lincoln was ahead of his time on this. He had the first cat in the White House. Ten other American presidents thought a furry, warm feline was a good idea. Presidential cat lovers include Rutherford B. Hayes, who had the first Siamese cat in the United States, and Bill Clinton, whose daughter's black-and-white cat, Socks, got so much mail—75,000 pieces a week—that the cat had its own zip code. Socks was also the first First Pet to have its own Web site.

what Kind of cat IS that?

For thousands of years, the striped tabby cat has been the most common domestic cat; it's found all over the world. People bred cats as early as the 14th century, but serious breeding efforts are not even 200 years old. Since cats, unlike dogs, didn't have a variety of jobs that required certain physical traits, there was never as much demand for a variety of cats.

siamese Cat

The Cat Fanciers' Association recognizes 41 breeds. You can buy a pedigree cat with folded ears, curled ears, wavy fur, no hair, bob tail, and no tail.

Sphynx cat

Manx cat

Tabby cat

So what kind of cat do 95% of American cat owners have? The ordinary, mixed-breed household cat.

Cornish Rex cat

If you have $50,000, you can clone a favorite pet cat. These two Bengal cat kittens, Tabouili and Baba Ganoush, are each clones. They were presented at the CFA cat show in 2004.

Scottish Fold cat

Felines were clean animals before Ed Lowe came along—but after he invented kitty litter, they were tidy cats! Before the 1940s, many people used ashes from fireplaces in their cat boxes. Then Lowe realized clay was a better bet: more absorbent, no soot. He drove around the country to stores and cat shows, selling brown bags of his kitty litter clay. By 1964, he had a brand name, Tidy Cat®, and a booming business.

PURINA

TIDY CATS

ODOR CONTROL

for MULTIPLE CATS

American Curl cat

Down, Boy!

Boxer

Imagine trying to train a bunch of cats...or even getting one cat to sit, stay, or heel. Good luck!

Unlike cats, dogs are animals that live in packs, like their wolf ancestors. They recognize a hierarchy with a leader and rules of behavior. They like to lick, nuzzle, wrestle, nip, and play with one another. In other words, dogs are social creatures like ourselves. They could adapt to living with us. We were just another kind of pack. That's why dogs make such great pets.

Mutt

By 9,000 years ago, *Canis familiaris*—the domestic dog—had spread all over the world. When dogs started living with humans, they redirected some of their pack behavior to people. A dog's owner was now the alpha, or lead animal in the pack. When dogs jump up and lick you, wag their tails like crazy, or roll over, they're showing you the respect that their wolf ancestors would have given the alpha animal in the pack. (Dogs do this to other dogs, too, once they've sniffed each other thoroughly to determine who's who in the canine pecking order.)

In a pack, wolves live and hunt as a group. They communicate with one another through sound and movement. They work cooperatively to get something done, such as catching an elk for dinner. They're responsive to one another and wisely stay clued in to the alpha wolf's mood. Wolves have good observation skills. They are very aware of body language, and can judge whether another wolf is aggresive or submissive. Dogs inherited these traits. They are remarkably sensitive to verbal, visual, or emotional cues from human beings. They're intelligent, with keen memories and even keener senses.

Bulldog

woof & waggle

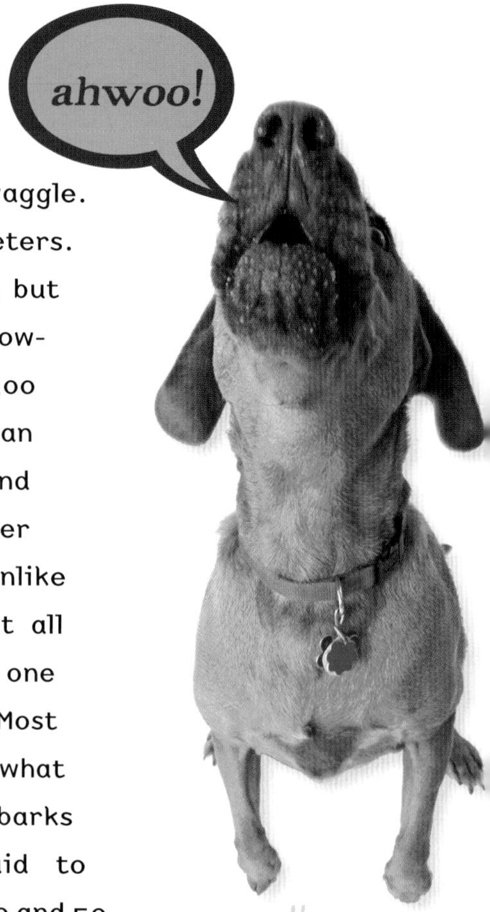

ahwoo!

Dogs aren't just all woof and waggle. They're living, breathing sense-o-meters. Puppies can't smell or hear at birth, but once they grow up, they're canine know-it-alls. Most dogs' sense of smell is 500 times greater than humans'. They can hear higher pitches than we can and hear sounds up to 40,000 vibrations per second, twice what we can pick up. Unlike their howling wolf ancestors, almost all domesticated dogs bark. Barking is one way dogs communicate. Most dog owners recognize what their dogs' different barks mean. Dogs are said to recognize between 40 and 50 of our verbal phrases.

huh?

Hound

Terrier

English Bulldog puppies

Please pick-up
after your pet.

Dogs must be on a
leash at all times.
M.C. 349-16/-11

woof!

Sheltie

Because they're pack animals, dogs like company. When a puppy is six to eight weeks old, it's ready to be socialized and learn about the family—animal or human—that it will join. Puppies also need to be housebroken. Their wolf ancestors would just poop on the go. Since the wolf pack traveled, they didn't have to worry about messing up their home. Pet dogs have to be taught excretory etiquette or how to "do their business" outside.

How a Dog works

Are you looking at me?

Eyes on either side of the head give most dogs a 240°–250° field of vision. We see about 70°. Most dogs don't have exceptional long-distance vision, but they see better than we do in low light.

You might think your dog looks cute in a red-and-green Christmas scarf, but he'll only see dark-and-white shades. Dogs are red-green color-blind. They see blue and yellow; almost everything else is pale.

Yum!

Dogs have taste buds for sweet, sour, and bitter flavors. A taste bud at the tip of the tongue tests out the taste of water.

Chomp!

Dogs have incisors; sharp, pointed canine teeth; and molars. All dogs have 42 teeth. They can chomp down with an average force of 150 to 200 pounds per square inch.

Some dogs try to move their facial muscles to mimic human smiles with a doggy grin.

There's a vomeronasal sense organ at the top of the mouth. It processes chemical information from air the dog sucks in.

The nose knows.

To a dog, "What's that smell?" is the same question as "What's going on?" Dogs sniff out information about the world. A dog has 200 million scent receptors in its nose and the roof of its mouth. (We have 5 million.) These receptors send information to the olfactory bulb, the brain's scent-processing center. Dog olfactory bulbs are four times the size of ours.

A dog's nose is wet because moisture helps conduct smells.

On your mark...get set...tiptoe!

Dogs walk on their toes; it's easier for them to run that way. There are four toes on each paw and thick, leathery pads to protect their feet; there's a dewclaw a little further up the leg.

say what?

A dog can move its ears to hear better. It's like tuning in the radio. There are 17 muscles in a dog's ears, which rotate the ears or move them up, down, or forward. Dogs with pricked or erect ears hear better than dogs with pendant or floppy ears.

tales tails tell

Long, short, fluffy, curly, clipped: Dog tails may look different, but they are all canine signals:

wagging = excitement

upright = alert, interested

hanging low = submissive

tucked in = afraid

upright & stiff or pointed straight out = Watch out! This dog is angry or aggressive.

fido was here.

Male dogs mark their territory with urine, which contains their own particular chemical scents. Of course, other dogs are doing the same thing, so male dogs spend a lot of time respraying the same spots.

There are scent glands on either side of a dog's anus. That's why dogs smell under each other's tails. A good sniff gives them information about who a dog is, where it's been, and what its rank is in the canine world.

mongrel vs. Pedigreed

Thousands of years ago, people realized dogs were excellent guardians, skilled hunters, and understanding pets. What more could you ask for?

How about a bigger, or smaller, or faster, or furrier, or fiercer, or sweeter dog?

How about a dog with long legs, or short legs, or webbed feet?

How about a dog that fits in a teacup? Or one that stands seven feet tall on its hind legs?

Today there are 400 recognized breeds of *Canis familiaris*, many of them bred in the last few centuries. Kennel clubs register purebred dog breeds according to very strict standards and require proof of a dog's lineage. But dog breeding itself goes way back.

The paw prints of canine history aren't always easy to track. Ancient peoples didn't have kennel club rules. They didn't use pedigree breed names: Greyhounds were any kind of big, fast hunting dog; Mastiffs were any kind of huge, tough pooch.

French Bulldog

Schnauzer

Alaskan Malamute

Basset Hound

Bernese Mountain Dog

Domesticated dogs were mongrels for centuries, and there have been plenty of mutts throughout history. Most were working animals; some were family pets.

There are clues in art, architecture, and literature about when certain kinds of dogs first appeared. Sometimes there are even historical records. But one thing is clear: When people saw something they liked in a dog, they wanted more of it in the next litter!

Good Breeding

Five thousand years ago, maybe more, people started selectively mating dogs. As trade routes developed linking different cultures, dogs became trade goods, which meant new breeding opportunities with the canines in distant lands. Wars were waged and empires rose and collapsed. To the victor fell the spoils—including dogs. More breeding opportunities.

Springer Spaniel

Golden Retriever

Dalmatian

English Bulldog

People in power wanted canines with class. In many countries, laws were passed that said who could own what dogs. Valuable dogs, like hunting breeds, or some of the aristocratic "toy" dogs from Asia, were strictly for nobility. The secrets of breeding these dogs, like the dogs themselves, were closely guarded.

Here's a look at some dog breeds that were beloved, envied, treasured, even horded through history. Many of them are among today's favorite pet pooches.

Latin bandleader Xavier Cugat often tucked one of his Chihuahuas into his coat pocket before getting ready to rhumba. Movie star Marilyn Monroe called hers Choochoo. Madonna and Jennifer Lopez own the minidogs. Pop singer Britney Spears was once photographed with her Chihuahua, which sported a $100,000 diamond dog collar.

Yo Quiero Chihuahua

Before Christopher Columbus hit the beach in 1492, dogs were the only domesticated animals most Native Americans owned. Dog remains found in Utah date back to 8000–7000 BC. Mayan ceramics from Mesoamerica show women fondly holding small dogs, probably pets. In South America, ancient Peruvians buried dogs wrapped in decorated cloths nearly 3,000 years ago.

North American Indians bred and traded dogs, from coyotelike creatures to smaller, pug-nosed pups. Most North American dogs had to earn their keep by hunting or helping with chores, although sometimes women and children kept small dogs as pets. In some wealthy tribes of the Pacific Northwest, pet dogs were canine status symbols. They showed that a person was

60

rich enough to feed a useless animal...*and* didn't need to eat it!

Cooked dog was part of the diet of some farming tribes; other Native American hunters wouldn't touch these hot dogs. Some tribes only ate dog during sacred ceremonies. (Ideas about eating dog vary around the world.)

The Maya, Aztecs, and Incas raised a hairless little dog with pointed ears. They were often used as canine heating pads (no hair, remember? Just nice warm, soft skin) or as Band-Aids, since it was believed they could help heal wounds. Now called by its Aztec name, Xoloitzcuintli, this ancient breed is the national dog of Mexico.

Stone carvings from the 9th century show that the Toltecs and Aztecs, ancient people of Mexico, bred a small dog called a *Techichi*. *Techichi* were long-haired dogs that didn't bark. They were popular pups: Wealthy Mesoamericans doted on them as pets; poor people ate them. The Aztecs thought a bluish-looking *Techichi* was sacred; they sacrificed yellow ones when someone died. *Techichi* were believed to be guides to the underworld who could help their owners. They were also probably the ancestors of Chihuahuas.

Chihuahuas are named after the Mexican state where they were found in the 19th century. American tourists liked the tiny dogs and started bringing them home. In the 20th century, they became a major media dog when Taco Bell used a hyper Chihuahua to hawk its fast food. In 2003, Chihuahuas made the American Kennel Club's top-ten list of most-popular breeds.

The Chihuahua is a perfect city pet: A dog that's

Chihuahua

only six inches high and weighs less than six pounds doesn't take up a lot of room in an apartment. With their little heads, big ears, and soulful eyes, Chihuahuas are so cute and easy to carry around, they've practically become a fashion accessory!

A disc from c. 2950 BC shows Egyptian hunting hounds.

King Tut's Pups

Most people associate cats with the ancient Egyptians, but dogs were actually their main family pets. The canines were a part of the household and had their own names, unlike Egyptian cats.

The Egyptians raised several kinds of dogs and were especially famous for their Gazehounds. Gazehounds are tall, sleek, swift hunting dogs, which look for their prey rather than sniff it out. Dog mummies and tomb art show that the Egyptians prized these dogs. Their elegant Gazehounds are pictured more often than other Egyptian dogs. There are drawings and carvings of Gazehounds dating from around 2900 BC.

Egyptian Gazehounds included Salukis, the oldest-known breed of dog. Salukis may have been first bred by Arab tribesmen nearly 8,000 years ago. But the most famous Egyptian Gazehound was the Greyhound, the prince of dogs.

Greyhounds were raised exclusively by the pharaohs and royal families of Egypt, who recorded the dogs' births and deaths. The ancient Greeks traded with the Egyptians for Greyhounds. Roman soldiers probably brought Greyhounds back from Egypt, and the breed spread through the Roman Empire.

Greyhounds: from Royal Courts to Racetracks

For centuries, Greyhounds were the dogs of choice for the world's upper class. King Charles IX of France so loved his Greyhound, he fed it sweets and biscuits by hand; when the dog died, he had a pair of hunting gloves made from its remains.

Renaissance artists painted portraits of aristocrats with their Greyhounds. The dogs symbolized chivalry and nobility. By the 15th and 16th centuries, the rich were entertaining themselves with Greyhound racing, a sport that still exists today.

Miniature Greyhounds became wildly popular dogs at court from the 17th century on. During the course of his life, King Frederick II of Prussia owned 35 of them. He pampered them with their own silk-covered chairs. In 1745, Frederick's favorite dog was captured during the Seven Years' War. He negotiated its release as part of a prisoner-of-war exchange. Queen Catherine the Great of Russia owned Greyhounds. So did Queen Victoria of England.

Greyhounds probably traveled

Greyhound

to the Americas in the early 16th century with Spanish explorers. U.S. cavalry commander George Custer, who made his famous "last stand" at Little Bighorn, loved hounds. He had a pack of 40, including Greyhounds.

Greyhounds can run 40 mph and deliver a crushing bite on the move. They easily took care of the jackrabbits and coyotes that plagued 19th-century farmers in the Midwest.

In 1920, the first official Greyhound racetrack opened in the United States. Today, many people keep pet Greyhounds that have been rescued or retired from racing.

Canine Secrets of the Orient

When you spot a Lhasa Apso, the last thing you'd think is "guard dog." You'd probably wonder how this little pup sees anything from underneath all that hair.

But the Lhasa Apso is just one

Lhasa apsos once guarded palaces such as this one in Tibet.

Lhasa Apso

Shih Tzu

of the many small breeds of dog that came out of Asia centuries ago and have long, distinguished histories. Apsos came from Lhasa, the sacred city of the Dalai Lama in Tibet, a rugged, isolated country in the Himalayan Mountains. Though only 10 inches tall, this furry little dog has excellent hearing. It guarded the inside dwellings of Lhasa (just in case, though, there was a huge Mastiff tied up on the outside walls).

China was the ancient center of the small-dog world from at least 500 BC, maybe earlier. Pugs, Pekingese, Chin, and Shih Tzu were bred in monasteries, imperial households, or the Forbidden City in Peking, now called Beijing. They were royal gifts among the emperors in China, Korea, and Japan.

Japanese Chin

Sturdy, snarfling, snub-nosed little Pugs with their curled pig tails guarded ancient temples in Tibet and China as early as 400 BC. By the 8th century, they were popular dogs in the Chinese imperial court; by 900, they were fashionable in Japanese courts, too. The Japanese traded with the Dutch, and the little Pug headed west. William, Prince of Orange, made the Pug the official dog of the Netherlands in the 16th century, after one foiled an assassination attempt on him. Soon the bullish little dogs were all the rage in European courts. Napoleon's wife Josephine had Pugs. One bit the pint-sized emperor on their wedding night. British queen Victoria owned 36 Pugs in her lifetime.

wang wang

bow-wow

woet

ouah ouah

Kyan Kyan

Pug

Pekingese

A Peek at the Pekes

It's hard to imagine how one pooch can be both a "lion dog" and a "sleeve dog," but that aptly describes the Pekingese. Its ancestors may have been pugs crossed with Maltese, small dogs that the Greeks and Romans traded for Chinese silk in the 2nd century BC.

Complicated ancient breeding techniques, such as smushing a puppy's muzzle and endlessly massaging it, were believed to help create the Pekingese's feathery fur around its really flat, broad-nosed face. The idea was to make the Peke look like a lion. Chinese legend tells of a great lion that fell in love with a small monkey. The lion asked the god of animals to shrink him but let him keep his lionhearted nature. The offspring of the shrunken lion and the monkey was the Pekingese. The Pekingese were the secret of the imperial Chinese court. Stealing one meant execution. In 1860, the British invaded Beijing, looted the royal palace, and took five Peke pups to England. The Chinese empress later sent a black Pekingese to President Teddy Roosevelt's daughter.

The famous psychologist Sigmund Freud owned a Chow. It sat in on his patient sessions. When the 50-minute session was up, the Chow headed for the door. Freud celebrated his birthday with his dogs. It was birthday hats and cake all around!

Pekingese were sometimes used to announce the Chinese emperor with their sharp, piercing barks or to carry his train in their mouths. Really small Pekes that could be carried around in the long sleeves of the Chinese nobility's robes were also greatly valued. The imperial Pekingese had their own servants, who kept them pampered and perfumed and comfy on satin cushions. Some Chinese Pekes even had titles and noble rank.

The Chinese also raised larger hunting dogs, like Chows Chows. This woolly dog with a blue-black tongue dates back to 200 BC.

Cave Canem

The Romans were the top dog breeders of the ancient Western world. They loved their cute little lapdogs, and were known to bury these pets and even write funeral poems for them. But these world-conquering, sports-minded empire builders also really loved big dogs, such as Mastiffs, Greyhounds, or

The Romans came up with the original "beware of dog" sign. This one was found in Pompeii; it survived the eruption of Mount Vesuvius in 79 AD.

the enormous Irish Wolfhounds they got from the Celts.

Mastiffs are big, square-headed, muscular dogs that can weigh 200 pounds. They have guarded people and property for thousands of years. Mastiffs fought bravely during Julius Caesar's invasion of Britain in 55 AD. The Romans pitted them against gladiators for entertainment. And yet, these huge powerful beasts liked human contact. Roman families sometimes kept Neapolitan Mastiffs at home, as part of the household.

The Romans prized the giant dogs the Celts raised. These legendary "Hounds of Ireland" are the tallest dogs in the world. They had to be: Their prey were originally wolves and the great Irish elk, which stood seven feet at the shoulders and had 12-foot antlers.

Only Irish nobility were allowed to raise these fierce canine warriors. Irish Wolfhounds were treasured gifts and valuable trade items. Soon they were scarce in Ireland, so their export was banned in 1652. Maybe that's why George Washington had such a hard time getting one more than a hundred years later.

Irish Wolfhounds are three feet tall at the shoulder and can stand seven feet tall on their hind legs. Presidents Herbert Hoover and John F. Kennedy both had Irish Wolfhounds in the White House.

Hounds, Hot Dogs, & Spaniels

Many of the great dogs that spread throughout the Roman Empire became the popular breeds of royal hunting and racing dogs in the Middle Ages and Renaissance. The flap-faced, flap-eared Bloodhound that is everybody's favorite detective symbol comes from the Saint Hubert's hound, bred by French monks in the 8th century. So does the droopy-faced, bandy-legged Basset Hound, the "Hush Puppy" you may have seen on shoe boxes. The elegant Cocker Spaniel, with its silky coat and long, wavy-haired ears, originally hunted game birds. It's a member of the spaniel family, a group of breeds that goes back to the 13th century.

In 1952, Richard Nixon was running for vice president. There was a scandal about questionable cash gifts to his campaign. Nixon defended

President Richard Nixon and Checkers, probably the most famous Cocker Spaniel in the United States.

Dachshund

himself in a TV speech. He said Checkers had been a gift, too, but that his kids loved the pet, and "we're gonna keep it!" The pooch play for sympathy probably saved Nixon's political career.

You might call them "hot dogs," but *Dachshund* is German for "badger dog." This barrel-chested little dog that's now such a popular pet was a wily hunter bred in the 1400s. These waddling minihounds also amused the nobility by chasing and killing the rats that scurried through their palaces.

Good with Kids

If you look at recent American Kennel Club lists of the 10 most popular dog breeds, you'll see plenty of canines, such as Golden Retrievers, Terriers, and Poodles, that used to have jobs, beyond being prizewinners or favorite pets, that is.

Before they became the model "family dog," Golden Retrievers were bred in 19th-century Scotland as bird hunters. In the 1920s, a wealthy Indian maharaja threw a lavish wedding for his Golden Retrievers. The doggy bride wore a coat and jeweled necklace; the groom was wrapped in a silk cummerbund; 250 dogs in fancy-dress were their attendants. President Gerald Ford's Golden, Liberty, lived a bit more modestly in the White

President Ford and pooch in the oval office.

House in the 1970s, although the First Dog did have her own seal—her paw print—for fan mail.

Labrador Retrievers, also popular pets, probably find fetching a stick a lot more fun than hauling in heavy fishing nets, as their canine ancestors had to do. Labradors actually were first bred in Newfoundland, Canada, which is where the Newfoundland, a huge, web-footed bear of a dog, comes from. Meriwether Lewis, of Lewis-and-Clark fame, took his Newfie, Scannon, along on his famous exploration of the Louisiana Purchase in 1804.

Tough Little Terriers

Terriers are cute, spunky little dogs that will draw you right into the pet store. But don't be fooled: These adorable pets were bred to flush out foxes, kill rats, and chase rabbits. Sure, today's breed of Yorkshire Terrier has floor-length hair, usually has to wear a bow or barrette so it can see, and glides along like it has no feet. But the Yorkie's ancestors were terriers that British miners and weavers brought to work to kill rats in the coal mines and cotton mills.

Yorkshire Terrier

Another Terrier with long hair and hidden feet is the Skye Terrier. Smart dog! Alexander Graham Bell taught his Skye Terrier to talk by manipulating the pooch's lips and rewarding it with food. With Bell's help, the dog could say, "How are you, Grandmamma?" Bell was studying ways to help deaf people learn to speak.

The Jack Russell is a popular Terrier pup. This breed was started by an English minister in the mid-1800s. Pit Bulls are also Terriers, but because they're often abused and trained for fighting, or are involved in attacks on people and pets, they've earned a bad reputation.

Jack Russell Terrier

Poodle

Did You want that Dog Small, Medium, or Large?

How many other dogs come in three sizes: standard, miniature, and toy? That's how you pick your Poodle, a hunting dog bred in the 13th century, that has been the pet of kings, presidents, and movie stars. Poodles are incredibly intelligent and good swimmers—despite the weird haircuts they're often given. Some of them are good on a road trip, too. The American writer John Steinbeck took his Poodle, Charley, traveling. Man and dog hopped in a car and drove on a 10,000-mile tour of the United States, which became the subject of the book *Travels with Charley*. (Steinbeck's Poodle was classy: It only responded to commands in French!)

John and Charley

Every Dog Has His Day

Starring in the movies, being on TV, making headlines because you had puppies in the White House—all these things can make a particular dog breed really popular.

Loyal, courageous German Shepherds are famous for the work they do as police, rescue, and Seeing-Eye dogs. But they're also a popular breed of pet. Maybe Rin Tin Tin helped with that. This German Shepherd puppy was rescued by a U.S. soldier in France during World War I and taken to Hollywood. In the 1920s, Rin Tin Tin became a big movie star, earning $1,000 a week, good money for anybody at the time, never mind a dog. His offspring continued the heroic adventures of Rin Tin Tin, which also became a television show.

Collies come from a long line of herding dogs. In the 1860s, people bought these noble-

Lassie always saves the day. But Lassie was really a "laddie," a male dog named Pal. Male Collies have better-looking coats and are easier to work with than females. Pal's descendants played all the other Lassie roles.

looking long-haired dogs because Queen Victoria did. President Calvin Coolidge and his wife, Grace, kept two big white Collies, one of which wore big, fancy hats to garden parties at the White House.

But it was Lassie who put Collies on the map. This rough-haired Collie starred in the 1942 movie classic *Lassie Come Home*, which created a whole Lassie industry. There were more movies, a long-running TV series, and, of course, stuff: Lassie lunch boxes, Lassie comics, even Lassie rings.

Polka-Dot Pooches & Dancing Dogs

Dalmatians were working dogs in the 19th century. They ran ahead of the firemen's horse-drawn fire wagons. They barked madly to keep people and stray dogs out of the way so that they wouldn't scare the horses.

But once the first *101 Dalmatians* movie

Dalmatian

hit the big screen in 1961, people fell in love with the little polka-dot pooches. Pups of this popular dog are born pure white; their spots appear as they grow up.

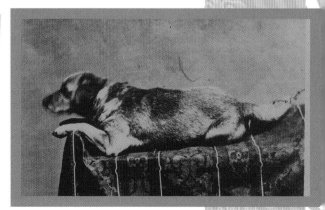

Beagle

No one's really sure exactly when Beagles first appeared in history, but it's a safe bet where the most famous Beagle of all lives: on top of a doghouse in the *Peanuts* comic strip. Charles Schulz's singing, dancing, lovable Snoopy has probably inspired countless kids to ask, "Can I get a Beagle?" Snoopy even has long, floppy ears like the real breed. Beagles are scent-hunting dogs; their ears brush along the ground and stir up smells, helping Beagles track prey.

President Lyndon Baines Johnson loved his two Beagles, Him and Her. He let them play in the Oval Office and trot into official receptions. LBJ got the thumbs-down from many people, though, for being photographed picking up the Beagles by their dangly ears.

Hail to the chief . . . Canine

If your owner gets elected president of the United States, your breed makes front-page news, too.

More than half of the U.S. presidents have been dog lovers. Our founding father, George Washington, is credited with breeding the first American

President Abraham Lincoln's pet mutt, Fido, was the first presidential dog ever photographed.

Foxhound. Thomas Jefferson instituted dog licenses by backing a law requiring dogs to wear collars with their owners' names.

When President Teddy Roosevelt was in office, all kinds of dogs, from a small, nippy Bull Terrier to a big old slobbery Saint Bernard, raced around the White House. The president's favorite was a mutt named Skip.

Americans loved President Franklin Roosevelt's black Scottie, which followed the president everywhere. Newsreels and newspapers were full of Fala: Fala in White House, Fala in the president's limousine, Fala at a press conference, Fala standing on hind legs when "The Star-Spangled Banner" played.

FDR and Fala on a road trip

President John F. Kennedy and his family always had a small pack of dogs. One was a fluffy little white puppy whose mother was one of the first dogs shot into space. Pushinka was a gift from the Soviet premier, Nikita Khrushchev, for JFK's daughter. Since the Cold War was on and the American and Russian governments didn't trust each other, little Pushinka was checked out by the army. You never know when a dog has bugs....

Pushinka takes a message for Caroline Kennedy

President Ronald Reagan hired an architect to design a house for his dog Rex. President Lyndon Baines Johnson also had a doghouse built at the White House. LBJ's had heat, lights, and air-conditioning.

Millie, President George H. W. Bush's Springer Spaniel, got a lot done in her one term as First Pet. She feuded with a Washington magazine over whether she was ugly or not; dictated her "dogobiography" to the First Lady; and had six puppies. Spot, one of Millie's pups, belonged to President George W. Bush, so it got another chance to live in the White House.

President Bill Clinton had a friendly, floppy, chocolate Labrador pup during his second term in office. Socks, the First Cat, already in residence, wasn't too happy about it. In the end, the dog was this man's best friend. Socks went to live with Clinton's press secretary.

Small Furry four-footers

It took a while for people to see small mammals like rabbits, ferrets, guinea pigs, hamsters, mice, rats, and gerbils and think, "Cute pet!"... instead of, "How tasty!"

Bountiful Bunnies

People have caught and kept rabbits since Roman times. But bunnies were first seriously bred by French monks around 600. They were basically meals in a hutch. Since rabbits reproduce rapidly, the meals kept coming. This made them attractive animals to take on board long sea journeys and explorations, too.

Rabbit keeping spread through Europe. By the 1800s, some people were interested in bunnies beyond dinner.

Dwarf Lop

Do your ears hang low? Yes, if you're a rabbit, like this dwarf lop. Lops were imported from Europe to the United States in the 1970s. Dwarf lops are one of the top rabbit breeds here.

They started breeding domestic rabbits as show animals or pets. Around 1888, the domestic rabbit made it to America—and made it big.

The Belgian hare set off a huge bunny craze at the end of the 19th century. The Belgian, which is really a rabbit, not a hare, was heavily promoted as a get-rich-quick opportunity. Americans paid as much as a $1,000 for these long-legged rabbits, whose offspring they planned to sell for meat. The market didn't pan out as planned, but people became more and more interested in rabbits as pets.

From the 1920s on, rabbit fanciers bred bunnies with different fur colors and patterns and even droopy, lop-eared rabbits.

There are now roughly five million pet rabbits hippity-hopping around homes in the United States.

Angora rabbits can produce two pounds of wool a year, which can be spun for use in clothes or blankets. They are one of the oldest breeds of rabbits and may have originally come from Turkey.

Angora

frisky ferrets

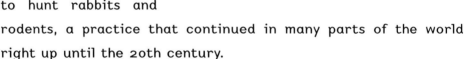

No one is quite sure exactly when people first domesticated these small, slinky animals that are in the same family as weasels and skunks. Ancient Greeks and Romans trained them to hunt rabbits and rodents, a practice that continued in many parts of the world right up until the 20th century.

From the seafaring Phoenicians on, ferrets were sailors' friends. They kept rodents from overrunning the ships. The first domestic ferrets probably sailed to America in the early 18th century. Ferrets even served in the Massachusetts colonial navy in the 1770s. In the 1900s, there were actually ferretmeisters in the United States. They'd come to your farm with their ferrets and let them loose on your rodent problem. In modern times, ferrets were used to pull wires and cables through pipelines, tunnels, and tight spaces for the oil, phone, and aircraft industries.

Ferrets are good workers, and they're also smart and affectionate. Some people preferred them as animal chums rather than as hunters. Queen Elizabeth I of England kept red-eyed, white-furred albino ferrets as pets in the 16th century. More than 200 years later, Queen Victoria also nuzzled up to the sleek animals.

Today, there are millions of pet ferrets in the United States—not bad for an animal that stinks!

When they're excited or threatened, ferrets give off a musky smell from their scent glands. Ferret fans overlook what they call this "distinctive odor" in favor of ferret fun. You can walk a ferret on a leash and teach it tricks like rolling over for treats. It will give you a kiss or nap on your lap. And if a ferret's in a really good mood, it just might puff up its fur, open its mouth wide, and crazily dance around sideways.

How Piggy Is a Guinea Pig?

True or false? Guinea pigs are so named because:

- They came from Guyana, a South American country where Dutch colonists found them in the 16th century.
- They once cost a guinea, a British coin.
- They squeal like pigs.

Answer: True? False? No one knows for sure why the furry little cavy (from *Cavia*, part of its scientific name) is called a guinea pig.

People in Peru and Bolivia raised guinea pigs for food nearly 5,000 years ago. In the 13th century, the Incas also used them for mystical purposes. The small rodents were thought to detect disease in the living by squeaking near an infected body part, and to help guide the dead to the next world.

Guinea pigs look like a one-piece animal: It's hard to tell where the head ends and the body begins. This animal's digestive system is really large so that it can process tough plant food; a guinea pig's back legs point sideways to fit around its big belly.

From the 15th century on, explorers, conquistadores, and sailors brought the cute little critters back to Europe, where they were treated as expensive, exotic pets at royal courts. The well-traveled guinea pig then came back to North America with the British colonists and ended up as dinner again.

But by the early 20th century, guinea pigs came into their own as pets. People started breeding them to get long hair, springy hair, wiry hair, crested hair, all kinds of fur color combinations, and even red eyes. Because they're so cuddly and easy to handle, guinea pigs have become really popular household pets.

Rodents with a Rep

Mickey and Minnie Mouse. Cinderella's mice. Stuart Little. Rodent heroes, every one of them. They've helped mice and rats overcome their bad reps.

The ancient Greeks, Romans, Chinese, and Japanese were okay with domesticating white mice, which were considered sacred or signs of good fortune. A rat is companion to the Hindu god Ganesh. But for centuries, most people thought of mice and rats as grain-snatching, diseased, devilish vermin;

nothing but good reasons to keep cats, dogs, snakes, ferrets, and mongooses.

In the 1700s, breeding unusually colored or albino mice as pets became popular in Japan. The practice spread to Europe by the 1800s. So did breeding rats for rat-and-dog fights, a popular 19th-century betting sport. Some of the better-looking—and *lucky*—rats escaped the fight pit and were bred for their exotic fawn or tortoiseshell-colored fur.

Pet mice are generally more timid than pet rats. Fancy rats are sociable critters. They'll play games, do tricks, even go for a walk. If they're happy, they'll let you know it—by grinding their teeth.

By 1895, the National Mouse Club (which included bred rats) was founded in England to encourage rodent appreciation. That appreciation ended in science labs in the United States, which is where most breeding took place. Today's fancy rats and fancy mice, the proper names for these pets, are the offspring of rodents bred mostly for experiments. They didn't really become popular pet-shop items in the United States until the 1950s.

Hairy Hoarders

The hamster is another small critter that got promoted from lab animal to beloved pet.

The chubby-cheeked, pert-eared golden hamsters scurrying around through the tunnels and tubes of their plastic hamster homes are the descendants of the mother of all domesticated hamsters.

A zoologist captured a wild female hamster and her 12 young near Mount Aleppo in Syria in 1930. The wild rodents had big eyes so that they could see in their underground burrows. Their fur was golden brown so that they blended in easily in the Syrian desert when they popped up for some food. The fur on their underbellies was white to reflect the desert heat. Some of the captured hamsters died or escaped; the few that survived were bred in a university lab in Jerusalem. By 1945, the pet industry had gotten hold of these energetic little fur balls. They were bred as show animals and advertised as household pets. Though hamsters are shy and nocturnal, people warmed to them because hamsters are hardy, easy to handle, and fascinating to watch. Luckily, once hamsters were a hit, there was no shortage of them. Female hamsters can birth up to 14 babies *ten times a year!*

Golden hamsters, sometimes called Syrians, aren't just golden anymore; they can be black, gray, orange, or piebald. There are also two other bred hamster species now kept as pets, the dwarf Russian and the Chinese hamster. The Chinese is a unique hamster

The word *hamster* comes from *hamstern*, German for "to hoard." Hamsters stuff food in cheek pouches that go all the way back to their shoulders, but wait until they are in a safe place to actually eat. Their wild ancestors had to do this: If the hamster didn't get back to its burrow quickly, *it* might become somebody's food.

because it has a long tail, unlike the little stubs at the end of most hamsters.

Here a Gerbil, there a Gerbil

If you were born in the 1970s or later, there's probably been a gerbil in your life. These small furry animals with tails nearly as long as their bodies are the rodents of choice in millions of homes and classrooms.

The Mongolian gerbil is the most common of these pets. Mongolian gerbils were captured and bred as lab animals by Japanese scientists in the 1930s. By the 1950s, labs in Europe and the United States were also working with the small rodents. Like hamsters, gerbils reproduce rapidly, so there were soon plenty of them available to pet stores.

Gerbils are cute, curious, and like company, so they usually don't live alone (which sometimes means more gerbils than you counted on!). Although they're only about four or five inches long, they can leap as high as two feet because of their powerful hind legs. And if they get mad or spot danger, they'll start thumping away with those hind legs.

fine-feathered friends

Parakeets

Nowadays if you've got $20, you can bring home a fine-feathered friend all your own. But for centuries, birds fluttered around only in the homes of the royal or wealthy. They were flying status symbols.

From the earliest times, people were amazed by beautiful creatures that flew, sang, even talked—and could be very tasty roasted. Cage birds spread throughout the world just like other captive animals did: They were trade goods or war booty.

Those able-bodied seamen, the Phoenicians, probably captured magnificent blue peacocks on their travels and brought them to Egypt. The Egyptians were avid avian fanciers; they started collecting birds around 4000 BC or earlier. Some were sent to the pharaohs' royal zoos. Egyptian art suggests people were fond of keeping doves and parakeets as pets. They also used homing pigeons as messengers.

Pretty Pollys

India was the land of fantastic birds. An Indian warrior-king from the 4th century BC had trained parrots to flock over his head whenever he made public appearances. Alexander the Great and his army invaded that country in 327 BC and brought back parrots, peacocks, and beautiful green-feathered, red-beaked ringneck parakeets.

The Greeks and the Romans adored these colorful birds. Rich Greeks were amused by the chatty avians and kept parrots, parakeets, and mynah birds as pets. Like the Egyptians, the Greeks also kept pigeons. Around 770 BC, these birds became flying headlines: The Greeks sent out homing pigeons with messages about who had won Olympic events.

A stern-looking imperial eagle was emblazoned on the Roman emperor's armor and other military paraphernalia, but the Romans also loved more entertaining birds such as parrots and parakeets. They kept their feathery pets in fancy cages, some made of silver, ivory, or tortoiseshell. They hired bird tutors to teach their parrots and ringneck parakeets to speak...in Latin, of course.

The peacock was a great prize in the ancient world. In the 10th century BC, King Solomon is thought to have brought the famous-tailed birds to Israel. Peacocks were decreed the national bird of India in 1963.

Wealthy Romans took great pride in their personal aviaries, although some of the birds that flew around a Roman garden eventually ended up in a Roman kitchen. Bird was a great delicacy, especially peacock, which was dished up in its own feathers. More enterprising Romans sold and traded imported birds across the empire. Parrots brought from Africa were especially in demand. You could also buy finches, robins, and mynah birds in the Roman markets.

The Aztec emperor Montezuma had a magnificent aviary in his palace zoo. It took 250 pounds of fish and who-knows-how-many millions of insects to feed his birds. When they molted, the feathers were gathered and used to make brilliant coats. But most ancient peoples of the Caribbean and Central and South America didn't bother with birdcages. They tamed brilliantly colored parrots and parakeets and let them fly around their homes, huts, or temples.

Canary

ſinging Like a canary

The Canary Islands off the northwest coast of Africa were a frequent port of call for Spanish and Portuguese sailors in the 1500s. They knew a good thing when they heard it: canaries!

Soon, hundreds of these adorable little birds were shipped back to Europe, but they were still so rare that only the rich could afford them. Canaries sang their sweet songs in ornate cages, some made of gold, others encrusted with precious jewels. By the 17th century, German bird breeders had hatched what became the world's favorite triller: the yellow canary.

Birds were like little music boxes in colonial America. Tuneful American birds such as cardinals and mockingbirds were exported to England. Meanwhile, rich colonists bought imported parrots, finches, mynah birds, and canaries.

Canaries were wildly popular in the 1800s, especially roller canaries. You could hear the long trills and low, soft notes of these songbirds in many a Victorian parlor. Budgerigars, the most common pet bird today, also became household items in the 19th century. The perky little parakeets were pretty much unknown outside of Australia until a naturalist brought them to England in 1840. The "budgie" breeding business soared.

first Birds

Singers, squawkers, talkers—they've all been the feathery friends of presidents and first ladies. Martha Washington was fond of her green parrot, though her husband George may not have been. Thomas Jefferson trained his mockingbird, Dick, to whistle along while the great statesman played the fiddle. When music hour was over, Jefferson climbed the stairs to bed, and Dick hopped right up after him. President William McKinley also had a musical bird. His parrot, Washington Post, sang "Yankee Doodle"—when the bird wasn't screeching "Oh, look at all the pretty girls." (President Andrew Jackson's parrot Poll wasn't so polite. It screamed obscenities at Jackson's funeral.)

Teddy Roosevelt, Jr., kept a blue macaw in the White House when his father was president.

First Lady Dolley Madison was famous for her wit, charm, and fashion sense. She found the perfect companion in a chatty green parrot, which was a big hit at presidential parties. When the British burned the White House during the War of 1812, Madison rescued the Declaration of Independence...and, of course, her beloved bird.

First Lady Grace Coolidge was a bit of a free bird. She let her canaries, mockingbird, parrot, and mynah bird wing their way around the White House. Not all of them were highfliers: The mynah bird liked to perch on people's heads, especially the poor housemaid who was trying to do her chores.

The last First Birds to flutter around the White House were the canary and parakeets that belonged to President John F. Kennedy's children. The canary got a most presidential burial...in the White House lawn.

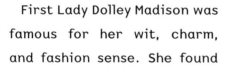

Parrot

finned favorites

What has fins instead of feet, scales instead of fur, and can blow bubbles under water? America's most populous pet: fish!

Fish outnumber all other household pets in this country; in fact, with 30,000 species, they're among the most numerous vertebrates on the planet. You'll find aquariums in nearly 13 million homes in the United States. If you ask these pet owners, "How do you like your fish?" the majority would say, "Fresh." Most home aquariums stock freshwater fish—185 million of them—compared to the 7 million fish bought for saltwater aquariums.

Goin' fishing

People started raising fish for food, not pets. The Sumerians stocked wild fish in outdoor ponds around 4,000 years ago. The ancient Egyptians

Goldfish

dug canals to channel wild fish from the Nile River into their gardens. The Egyptians relaxed by fishing in their canals, and they also recognized the peaceful pleasure of watching fish gracefully glide through their watery world. While most fish still ended up on the plate, some Egyptians kept species of outstanding beauty in outdoor pools, where these fish were fed, bred, and admired.

Fish farming really expanded in the Roman Empire during the 1st century BC. The Romans kept freshwater and saltwater fish, primarily for food. But wealthy Romans built fish tanks or *piscinari* right in their villas. Many of them regarded their fish as status symbols, rather than the daily catch. These Romans were snobbish about their fish collections; at one point, moray eels were all the rage.

Living Jewels

Nearly 2,000 years ago, Chinese farmers began keeping wild black or brown carp in their rice paddies for food, a practice that spread to Japan. Carp are the ancient ancestors of goldfish and koi, now the most popular pet fish in the world. By the 1500s, some Chinese and Japanese were keeping carp as decorative fish in pools.

In the 1800s, Japanese farmers in the Niigata area found red carp swimming in their rice paddies. A red fish was too special to eat! The Niigata farmers selectively bred carp with color mutations, creating koi, which is Japanese for "brocaded carp." They developed more than 100 kinds of koi, with incredible red, yellow, black, blue, white, or gray markings and coloration. The brilliant koi stayed in Niigata until 1914, when they were exhibited at the Great Tokyo Exhibition. Japanese emperor Hirohito was impressed by the Niigata "living jewels." Koi became the enormously popular national fish of Japan.

Raising, exhibiting, and judging koi, a fine art in Japan, is now an international movement. The fancy Japanese carp can grow up to three feet long, weigh up to 35 pounds, and live 30 years or more. Koi are carefully bred for their celebrated colors and unusual markings. However, one highly prized koi, a snowy white fish with a red circle on its head, was just born by chance and can't be bred.

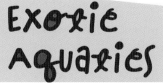

Koi

Exotic Aquatics

Meanwhile, international trade in the 17th, 18th, and 19th centuries brought exotic aquatics like the goldfish carp and the paradise fish from Asia to Europe and eventually to

America. In 1853, the first public aquarium opened in Regent's Park, London. It featured fish caught from British lakes and rivers. Three years later, the great American impresario P. T. Barnum opened the first U.S. public aquarium in New York City.

Pet-loving Victorians were fascinated by fish. Ornate home aquariums became popular among the rich. Goldfish bowls appeared in many a Victorian parlor. Enthusiastic fish collectors paid sailors to bring back exotic specimens from their voyages. But keeping fish was risky business.

For one thing, tropical aquariums were heated by open flames that warmed the tank's metal bottom. It was difficult to regulate the oxygen level and water temperature in these aquariums. Many fish were unfamiliar to their new owners. Who knew what these fish liked to eat? How much water they needed? How many were too many in a tank or fishbowl? There wasn't much information about how to care for fish; commercial fish food wasn't readily available.

View of the American Museum, Broadway, New York

the High-tech world of fish

But by the turn of the century, fish fans had made great improvements in food, filters, pumps, and the other amenities of aquarium life. Electricity certainly helped!

Technological advances in the 20th century spawned today's major pet-fish industry. Advances in air travel meant fish could be transported more safely and quickly worldwide. Pet fish today are mainly bred in Asia, Florida, and Hawaii. Many saltwater fish are captured in the wild, and there are environmental concerns about taking fish directly from open waters. Some species are endangered, and there are crackdowns on illegal fish sales.

The invention of silicone in the 1970s meant fish tanks could be sealed more efficiently. Air and filtration systems became more advanced. There are also a few U.S. veterinarian programs that specialize in ornamental-fish care—good news if you've just spent thousands of dollars buying a champion koi! Fish can even be operated on: A special machine pumps fluids into the fish's mouth and out its gills during surgery.

one Bright fish

Scientific research on fish began in the 4th century BC with Aristotle's formal study of 115 species of fish. By the 20th century, scientists had produced a new fish.

Scientists were trying to breed a fish that would glow when it swam into polluted water so that they could track the flow of toxins. GloFish went on the market in the United States in 2004. They're not for sale in all states because of controversies about genetically altered animals.

The GloFish lives up to its name: It glows . . . all the time! This wriggly little fluorescent zebra fish is the first bioengineered pet on the market. It's even patented! The tropical GloFish was developed at the University of Singapore nearly a decade ago. Scientists there injected a naturally occurring fluorescent gene from jellyfish and coral into the eggs of zebra danio fish. Presto! Bright little fish with great glows were born!

Everybody's favorite fish

Fluorescent may be the shiny wave of the future, but goldfish and koi are still today's most popular fish. A goldfish has even been a First Fish. President Ronald Reagan kept one in a tank with the presidential seal on it. Goldfish aren't just gold, either. The bug-eyed black moor, the blue-mottled shubunkin, and the calico telescope are all goldfish.

Whether they own a 99¢ neon or a $170,000 carp (the recent sale prize of a prizewinning koi), most fish people will tell you that watching fish is relaxing. Sure, fish are silent, mysterious, and glassy-eyed, but sit down in front of an aquarium for a while and you'll become quietly glassy-eyed yourself. And you'll feel good: Research shows that watching fish calms people. There are even some statistics that show that fish-owning students score higher on the SAT tests.

Goldfish

seales & tails

slithering snakes

When its feeding directions read, "Eats mice, prekilled if possible," you know you gotta really want this pet.

Snakes aren't for the squeamish (and some snakes, like the poisonous ones, shouldn't be pets at all...duh!).

People have had a love-hate relationship with snakes for thousands of years. Egyptian pharaohs wore golden headdresses shaped like rearing cobras to symbolize their divine power; female Egyptian royalty sometimes wore real snakes as decorative armbands. Egyptian queen Cleopatra clasped an asp—

Pythons are fairly easygoing reptiles as snakes go. This one, the ball python, is a very popular pet because it only grows to five or six feet.

The caduceus, the symbol of doctors and medicine, is a staff with two snakes coiled around it.

which promptly bit her to death—when her kingdom was falling to the Roman army.

The ancient Greeks and Romans were known to keep the slinky reptiles as pets. One writer from the 1st century AD tells of seeing tame snakes slithering across tables and around the diners at a Roman banquet. Snakes were also believed to have healing powers. (That's what 19th-century American "snake-oil" salesmen claimed, too. They sold bottles of snake oil as supposedly surefire cures for arthritis and other kinds of ailments.)

Divine or Deadly

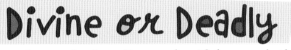

In ancient cultures in Africa and the Americas, snakes had divine status. The Maya and Aztecs worshipped Quetzalcoatl, a feathered serpent. A traditional sacred ceremony of the Hopi in the American Southwest involves a ritual dance with live snakes to appeal to rain gods and assure fertile crops. In India, snake-charming cobras is an age-old entertainment.

In the Bible, snakes were cursed for all time because Satan, in the form of a serpent, had tempted Adam and Eve in the Garden of Eden. This story shaped how the Western, Judeo-Christian

Cobras are hardly charming—one bite from this venomous serpent can kill you in 15 minutes. Snake charmers "hypnotize" this dangerous snake by swaying while they play their flutes. The cobra can't hear the high-pitched music, but follows the movement of the flute, which makes it look like the snake is dancing.

world thought of snakes for centuries. Snakes were usually symbols of all things cunning and wicked.

Still, there are millions of snake lovers who enjoy keeping them as pets. There's even been a First Snake in the White House. President Teddy Roosevelt's daughter, Alice, owned a green garter snake, Emily Spinach, who'd pop up here and there as a serpentine surprise.

Favorite pet snakes include corn snakes, black rat snakes, king snakes, boas, and pythons. When snake shopping, choose carefully: Some slinky slitherers really stretch out! The Burmese python can reach 15 feet in length.

Long-tailed Lizards

Wish you had a pet dragon? Lizards are about as close as you can get. These scaly, long-tailed reptiles look like they just scurried out of the dinosaur age.

Lizards were considered magical creatures for centuries. After all, it *is* pretty amazing to lose your tail and grow a new one or vividly change your skin color. The slinky reptiles were important creatures in the mythologies of many peoples, from the Bantu in Africa to the Maori in New Zealand. The Aboriginal people of central Australia believe a lizard ancestor freed the first people from being earthen lumps.

But in Central and South America, the common green iguana's nickname is *gallina de palo*—"chicken of the tree." Lizard is a delicacy there, and iguanas are raised on reptile farms as food.

There are more than 3,700 species of lizard, which makes them the biggest group in the reptile family. People are fascinated by ancient-looking lizards such as iguanas, anoles, bearded dragons, geckos, and chameleons. The number of people who own pet reptiles has greatly increased since the 1980s, and lizard fans are part of the reason why. Lizards seem like small, appealing pets, particularly for an apartment; however, as their owners soon find out, many of them, such as chameleons, require a great deal of care.

Common green iguanas—or to use their scientific name, *Iguana iguana*—are the most popular lizard pets in North America. And they're a whole lot of pet: These iguanas can grow up to five feet long and weigh nearly 20 pounds. They are usually pretty gentle and may even enjoy being petted under the chin or rubbed on the head. Iguanas are quiet, clean, and don't smell...but they're not exactly the chummiest animal pals.

Iguana

Way back in the 4th century BC, the ancient Greek scientist Aristotle was wondering what makes geckos stick. These amazing lizards can afix themselves to any surface, even glass! A gecko has millions of tiny hairs on each of its feet. These tiny hairs, called setae, end in miniature pads. Scientist think these microscopic pads are so close together that their sticking power is strong enough to counteract the force of gravity.

Geckos are also one of the few lizards that aren't silent. They chitchat with one another, making a "geck-o, geck-o" sound.

This leopard gecko is even more unusual. It stalks its prey—crickets and worms—and then pounces on it!

Leopard Gecko

Some scientific and animal welfare organizations, such as the Smithsonian National Museum of Natural History, advise against keeping reptiles as pets; ditto for amphibians such as frogs and turtles. These organizations are concerned about illegal or unhealthy shipping and handling practices in some parts of the exotic pet industry. They also feel people don't always realize what they're getting into when they take home these pets and are then unable to care for them properly. That's how you end up with a caiman swimming around in New York's Central Park or pythons and boas slinking through the Florida Everglades.

Members of the pet industry disagree. Some of them think consumer education and better business practices can make the reptile trade safe and environmentally sound.

Cricket

Eternal Pets

PRESIDIO OF SAN FRANCISCO PET CEMETERY

If you've ever buried a goldfish in the backyard, you're carrying on a tradition that's thousands of years old. From Egypt to the Americas, people have buried animals as part of sacred rituals (although sometimes "buried" really meant "sacrificed"), or to make sure the critters were around to help their human owners in the next life, or maybe just because the pet was so beloved in this life

Many ancient cultures, including the Aztec, Mayan, and North American Indian, believed dogs guided souls to or through the afterlife. Scientists have found the carefully placed remains of dogs in Native American burial sites in Illinois, Missouri, Tennessee, and Kentucky that date to between 6400 and 3000 BC. The Aztecs cremated a dog so that it could continue guarding and guiding its dead master.

GYPSY
1962 — 1976
THE CAT WHO

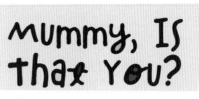

Mummy, Is that You?

When a pet died in ancient Egypt, all the people in the household shaved their eyebrows (for a cat), or their heads and whole bodies (for a dog) in mourning. The family pet was often mummified and buried in the family tomb, along with its owners. The Egyptians believed their animals would trot along with them in the afterlife. Sacred pets were also embalmed and buried in the great Egyptian animal necropolises, or cemeteries: dogs at Cynopolis, cats at Bubastis, each of which held thousands of mummies.

In the mid-19th century, 300,000 mummies were found in a cat cemetery in Beni Hasan, Egypt. Twenty tons, nearly all of these ancient remains, were shipped to Liverpool, England, and sold for fertilizer. The auctioneer is said to have used a mummified cat for his gavel!

When it comes to mummies, the Egyptians ruled. They oiled, waxed, wrapped, and preserved everything from bulls to beetles. As early as 1000 BC there were animal cemeteries along the Nile. Egyptian favorites—dogs and cats—were often embalmed and decorated with gold or turquoise jewelry. Their coffins were paraded through the streets before being buried or entombed.

Gone, But Not forgotten

The ancient Chinese also had pet cemeteries. They honored their dead dogs with marble, ivory, silver, and gold tombstones. In 1028

106

BC, they began the custom of burying the royal Pekingese when the emperor died. (By the 20th century, the dogs got off easier. When the dowager empress of China died in 1908, her favorite Peke only had to lead the funeral procession.)

Some wealthy ancient Romans went all out for their dearly departed pets. They built burial vaults, had sad songs or poems written in their pets' memories, and inscribed loving tributes on their tombstones.

Through the centuries, the crowned heads of Europe kept up this tradition. They hired artists, sculptors, and poets to immortalize their pets with white marble tombs, elaborate mausoleums, carved granite headstones, bronze statues, or flowery phrases. Some rich or middle-class pet owners in the 19th century added a fussy Victorian touch: They laid out their dead pets on lacy pillows and had them photographed before burial.

modern mourning

When pets die today, they can still be treated as royally as they were in the past. Many people spend hundreds or thousands of dollars memorializing pets that have passed on. There are about 600 pet cemeteries in the United States. The oldest one still operating, the Hartsdale Pet Cemetery in New

York, opened in 1896. The ashes or remains of more than 70,000 pusses, pooches, birds, bunnies, and even a lion cub are buried there.

Pet burials or cremations involve many choices: Should the coffin be plywood, oak, or cherry? Silk- or satin-lined? Should the tombstone be marble or granite? A poem, a photo, or both on it? Should there be a funeral? A viewing? Flowers? Music?

Some people like to keep their pets closer to home, so they get their deceased animals freeze-dried. After the pet dies, its body is frozen, specially treated, and posed as the animal looked in real life. The prepared body is then put in a special sealed vacuum chamber, where all the moisture is removed from the body to preserve it. The freeze-dried pet—body, fur, and all—will sit, lie down, or be curled up asleep for forever.

One U.S. company will mummify dearly departed pets. After being wrapped in linens and treated with oils and spices, the mummy is placed inside a bronze or gold-leaf mummy case shaped like the pet owner's dog, cat, or bird.

Some high-tech pet memorials don't need bodies or burial grounds. There are several online pet memorials, including a Virtual Pet Cemetery, where beloved pets live on forever in cyberspace through testimonials and digital photos.

the End

Selected Bibliography

Books

Alderton, David. *A Birdkeeper's Guide to Pet Birds.* Morris Plains, NJ: Tetra Press, 1987.

———. *Dogs.* New York: Dorling Kindersley, 1993.

———. *The Small Animals Question and Answer Manual.* Hauppauge, NY: Barron's, 2001.

Beck, Alan, and Aaron Katcher. *Between Pets and People: The Importance of Animal Companionship.* West Lafayette, IN: Purdue University Press, 1996.

Brazaitis, Peter, and Myrna A. Watanabe. *Snakes of the World.* New York: Crescent Books, 1992.

Bryant, Mark. *Casanova's Parrot and Other Tales of the Famous and Their Pets.* New York: Carroll & Graf Publishers, 2002.

Budiansky, Stephen. *The Truth about Dogs.* New York: Viking Press, 2000.

Burghoff, Gary, et al. *The Wonderful Thing about Pets: Remarkable Stories about the Animals Who Share Our Lives.* Emmaus, PA: Rodale, 2000.

Caras, Roger A. *A Perfect Harmony: The Intertwining Lives of Animals and Humans Throughout History.* New York: Simon & Schuster, 1996.

Carson, Gerald. *Men, Beasts, and Gods: A History of Cruelty and Kindness to Animals.* New York: Charles Scribner's Sons, 1972.

Chrystie, Frances N., updated by Margery Facklam. *Pets: A Comprehensive Handbook for Kids.* 4th rev. ed. Boston: Little, Brown, 1995.

Clark, Kenneth. *Animals and Men: Their Relationship as Reflected in Western Art, from Prehistory to the Present Day.* New York: William Morrow, 1977.

Clutton-Brock, Juliet. *Domesticated Animals from Early Times.* Austin: University of Texas Press, 1981.

Comfort, David. *The First Pet History of the World.* New York: Fireside, 1994.

Coren, Stanley. *The Pawprints of History.* New York: The Free Press, 2002.

Davis, Gibbs. *Wackiest White House Pets.* New York: Scholastic, 2004.

Edwards, Alan. *The Ultimate Encyclopedia of Cats, Cat Breeds, and Cat Care.* New York: Lorenz Books, 1999.

Ernst, Carl H., and George R. Zug. *Snakes in Question: The Smithsonian Answer Book.* Washington, DC: Smithsonian Institution Press, 1996.

Fireman, Judy, ed. *Cat Catalog: The Ultimate Cat Book.* New York: Workman, 1976.

Flank, Lenny, Jr. *Snakes: Their Care and Keeping.* New York: Howell Book House, 1998.

Franklin, Adrian. *Animals and Modern Cultures: A Sociology of Human-Animal Relations in Modernity.* Thousand Oaks, CA: SAGE Publications, 1999.

Fudge, Erica. *Animal.* London: Reaktion Books, 2002.

Hanna, Jack with Hester Mundis. *Jack Hanna's Ultimate Pet Guide.* New York: Putnam, 1996.

Henninger-Voss, Mary J. *Animals in Human Histories: The Mirror of Nature and Culture.* Rochester, NY: University of Rochester Press, 2002.

Hoage, R. J., ed. *Perceptions of Animals in American Culture.* Washington, DC: Smithsonian Institution Press, 1989.

Jes, Harald. *Lizards in the Terrarium.* Hauppauge, NY: Barron's, 1987.

Kelly, Niall. *Presidential Pets.* New York: Abbeville Press, 1992.

Lewinsohn, Richard. *Animals, Men, and Myths: An Informative and Entertaining History of Man and the Animals Surrounding Him.* New York: Harper, 1954.

Loxton, Howard. *99 Lives: Cats in History, Legend and Literature.* San Francisco: Chronicle Books, 1998.

MacDonogh, Katharine. *Reigning Cats and Dogs: A History of Pets at Court Since the Renaissance.* New York: St. Martin's Press, 1999.

Mattison, Chris. *Snake: The Essential*

Visual Guide to the World of Snakes. New York: DK Publishing, 1999.

Méry, Fernand. The Life, History and Magic of the Cat. New York: Grosset & Dunlap, 1968.

———. The Life, History and Magic of the Dog. New York: Grosset & Dunlap, 1968.

Necker, Claire. The Natural History of Cats. New York: Dell Publishing, 1977.

Page, George. Inside the Animal Mind. New York: Doubleday, 1999.

Preece, Rod. Animals and Nature: Cultural Myths, Cultural Realities. Vancouver, BC: UBC Press, 1999.

Rowan, Roy, and Brooke Janis. First Dogs: American Presidents and Their Best Friends. Chapel Hill, NC: Algonquin Books, 1997.

Sayer, Angela. The Complete Book of the Dog. New York: W. H. Smith Publishers, 1987.

Schwartz, Marion. A History of Dogs in the Early Americas. New Haven, CT: Yale University Press, 1997.

Serpell, James. In the Company of Animals: A Study in Human-Animal Relationships. New York: Basil Blackwell, 1986.

Shuttlesworth, Dorothy Edwards. Pets and People: How to Understand and Live with Animals. New York: Dutton, 1975.

Siino, Betsy Sikora. You Want What for A Pet?! A Guide to 12 "Alternative" Pets. New York: Howell Book House, 1996.

Spignesi, Stephen. The Cat Book of Lists: Facts, Furballs, and Foibles from Our Favorite Felines. Franklin Lakes, NJ: New Page Books, 2001.

Squire, Dr. Ann. 101 Questions and Answers about Pets and People. New York: Atheneum, 1988.

Szatsz, Kathleen. Petishism: Pets and Their People in the Western World. New York: Holt, Rinehart and Winston, 1969.

Thomas, Elizabeth Marshall. The Hidden Life of Dogs. Boston: Houghton Mifflin, 1993.

Tulin, Melissa S. Aardvarks to Zebras: A Menagerie of Facts, Fiction, and Fantasy about the Wonderful World of Animals. New York: MJF Books, 1995.

Vriends, Matthew. Simon & Schuster's Guide to Pet Birds. New York: Fireside, 1985.

Wells, Ken, ed. Herd on the Street: Animal Stories from The Wall Street Journal. New York: Free Press, 2003.

Wright, John C. with Judi Wright Lashnits. Ain't Misbehavin': The Groundbreaking Program for Happy, Well-Behaved Pets and Their People. Emmaus, PA: Rodale, 2001.

Periodicals

"In the Company of Animals (Conference Proceedings)." Social Research: An International Quarterly of the Social Sciences. 62, no. 3 (Fall 1995). New School for Social Research, NY.

Society & Animals: Journal of Human-Animal Studies 3, no. 2 (1995); 6, no. 1 (1998).

Glenn, Johsua. "Wild at Heart: How Pets Make Us Human." Utne Reader 73 (Jan.-Feb. 1996).

Media

Dogs and More Dogs, PBS/NOVA video. 2004.

The Royals and Their Pets, PBS show. 2004.

Animal Planet (cable)
http://animal.discovery.com

Web Sites

American Pet Products Manufacturers Association. www.appma.org

The American Kennel Club. www.akc.org

The American Society for the Prevention of Cruelty to Animals (ASPCA). www.aspca.org

The Cat Fanciers' Association. www.cfa.org

The Humane Society of the United States. www.hsus.org

PetPlace.com
www.petplace.com

Index